Cradle of a Healthy Life

Cradle of a Healthy Life

EARLY CHILDHOOD AND THE WHOLE OF LIFE

Nine WECAN Conference Lectures
by Dr. Johanna Steegmans

with summaries of lectures
by Dr. Gerald Karnow

**WALDORF EARLY CHILDHOOD
ASSOCIATION OF NORTH AMERICA**

Cradle of a Healthy Life: Early Childhood and the Whole of Life
First English Edition
© 2012 Waldorf Early Childhood Association of North America
ISBN: 978-1-936849-04-8

This publication was made possible by a grant
from the Waldorf Curriculum Fund.

Dr. Steegmans's lectures were transcribed and edited by Lory Widmer.
We are grateful to Fiona Gold for sharing her audio recordings.

Waldorf Early Childhood Association of North America
285 Hungry Hollow Rd.
Spring Valley, NY 10977
845-352-1690
info@waldorfearlychildhood.org
www.waldorfearlychildhood.org

For a complete book catalog, contact WECAN or visit our online store:
store.waldorfearlychildhood.org

Contents

Lectures by Dr. Johanna Steegmans
CRADLE OF A HEALTHY LIFE

Introduction by Annie Gross 9
Lecture 1 • *The First Three Years, Part I* 11
Lecture 2 • *The First Three Years, Part II* 25
Lecture 3 • *The First Three Years, Part II* 37
Lecture 4 • *Birth of the Imagination, Part I* 53
Lecture 5 • *Birth of the Imagination, Part II* 65
Lecture 6 • *Birth of the Imagination, Part III* 77
Lecture 7 • *Birth of the Etheric, Part I* 83
Lecture 8 • *Birth of the Etheric, Part II* 95
Lecture 9 • *Birth of the Etheric, Part III* 109

Lectures by Dr. Gerald Karnow
SUMMARIES BY NANCY BLANNING

Introduction by Nancy Blanning 123
Year 1 • *Living and Working with So-Called Difficult Children*
        Part I 125
        Part II 131
Year 2 • *Developing the Eyes to See* 141
Year 3 • *Deepening Our Capacities to Meet the Children in Our Care*. . 147

Bibliography

Dr. Steegmans's Lectures 157
Dr. Karnow's Lectures 159

The content of this book comes from two three-year sequences of keynote conference lectures. Dr. Steegmans's nine lectures were transcribed from audio recordings and edited for this publication, preserving the conversational style of the original talks, including comments and questions from the audience.

Dr. Karnow also gave nine lectures over a three-year period. These were not recorded or transcribed, but were summarized by Nancy Blanning from her own notes for publication in Gateways, *the newsletter of the Waldorf Early Childhood Association of North America. The written style of this section is thus much more condensed.*

Introduction
LECTURES BY DR. STEEGMANS

There were, of course many invisible threads woven over time, by our predecessors, that led to the publication of these lectures. However, here is my personal account of how the following lectures came about.

When I moved to the west coast over seven years ago, one of the things I missed most, apart from beloved family, friends and colleagues, was the WECAN East Coast February Conference. For many years, sometimes as many as thirteen of us early childhood faculty members at Toronto Waldorf School would pile into a van and drive for twelve hours to Spring Valley, New York. It was, without exception, always worth the drive even if it meant negotiating many snowstorms. Memories of the nourishing and inspiring contents of these conferences, as well as the deepening of collegial relationships, were the inspiration to create a similar activity here in the Pacific Northwest. A wish to support a pedagogically and socially enriching experience was incarnating.

In February 2008, during the AWSNA Regional Conference at Whatcom Hills Waldorf School in Bellingham, Washington, Holly Koteen-Soulé, Robin O'Brien and I (Pacific Northwest WECAN Regional Reps) met to talk about our region. Upon learning that there is more Waldorf activity in this region than anywhere else in North America, including thirty home-based programs in the Portland area alone, we wondered how WECAN might reach out in support of this important work, and at the same time create an opportunity for all the early childhood teachers and caregivers in the region to connect.

Holly approached Joseph Doucette from AWSNA and he agreed to our request to add an early childhood event before the February 2009 AWSNA Regional Conference. Our immediate and collective wish was to invite Dr. Johanna Steegmans to be our first keynote speaker. She accepted our invitation with one condition: that she could work with us for three consecutive years, leading us on a path of spiritual-scientific investigation of the first seven years of life. Needless to say, we were thrilled.

And so it was that the Eugene Waldorf School graciously hosted the first Pacific Northwest WECAN February Conference, followed in 2010 by Whidbey Island Waldorf School and finally in 2011 by Whatcom Hills Waldorf School. The theme of the first year centered on the formative experiences of the first three years, the second year on the "birth of the imagination" in the middle period of early childhood, and the final year on the "birth of the etheric" in the final years before school entrance.

Over the course of these three years, Dr Steegmans, out of her personal spiritual-scientific research, study, and professional practice, offered each of the eager and enthusiastic attendees many opportunities to expand and deepen their understanding of the developing human being. She created wonderful imagery of these tender years and at every turn was able to draw corollaries with various stages in human development. Woven into these descriptions she reminded us again and again that the element of self-development is an essential aspect of our pedagogical work.

Along with this profound pedagogical substance, a new social tapestry was being woven. At regular intervals Dr. Steegmans warmly included the audience by inviting comments and questions. She helped to deepen our interest not only in our own pedagogical striving, but just as importantly, in each other and in each other's work.

I am deeply grateful for the generosity of many who made these three conferences possible, and that they are now being made available for continued reading and study.

—Annie Gross

The First Three Years
PART I

It is really interesting to me that in the almost forty years that I have been around children, I know less and less. The words "the mystery of the young child" become more and more reality for me. At first it was a concept, and then it was a feeling, and now I know: the child, the soul/spirit just incarnated into a new body, is really a mystery. And this mystery is one we cannot solve by having dead concepts. We actually can only solve it by being with the children, because the answer to this mystery is in the child him- or herself, not in our concepts.

Now, since you challenged me to bring something new, I've been reading a lot of research. AWSNA has many great research papers out, and since I read German I can also read what is coming out of the German research in Europe. Very interesting things.

And then I go back to Rudolf Steiner's words. I read *The Spiritual Guidance of the Individual and Humanity*, a little book about how we learn to walk, talk, and think. And there are very precious lectures in the book that was translated as *Soul Economy*. Rudolf Steiner speaks about the wholeness of life, from birth all the way to age twenty-one. Or I look into *The Education of the Child*. Slowly I understand that through his way of speaking, Rudolf Steiner speaks words that leave us completely free. Because what I read twenty years ago and what I read today is very different. It's the same words, but they slowly, slowly start to unfold.

So he didn't give us the facts right away; as with the young child, we have to read them, live them, experience them, and then there is something new in the same sentences. And that is wonderful. That is writing out of freedom.

For Rudolf Steiner it was paramount that we leave children free to become who they want to be, who they came to become. There are other beautiful forms of education, but this urge to be *free* is quite unique to Waldorf education. And so as adult educators, as parents, teachers, caregivers, we need to develop ourselves more and more so that what we give to the child is more and more out of our time. There are things that are timeless, like learning to walk, to talk, and to think, but then the world changes, and children need to feel the world, the changing world, in us— always fresh, every day fresh. The way we are in the world is important for the children when they meet us.

So I will now talk for a short while, and then stop for a moment so that you can share the thoughts and ideas that come to you while I speak. That takes some courage, to get up and speak, but please do so because then we can weave something new, not just a lecture that gives you the newest facts about child development.

What I want to do in these two days is to make the bridge from the just-incarnating child, the just-incarnating soul/spirit, to the time in our life when we become free of the necessities of our destiny: that is around 63 years. Not many of us are 63; I am almost getting there, and I'm beginning to realize how it mirrors the early years, and out of this mirroring actually to understand the young child better and better. So I would like to show how this later time in our lives mirrors the early times. I will also look at how the early times also are mirrored in the twenty-first year of life, when the young person goes out into the world, and how they again are mirrored at 42.

So this is what I would like to do in choosing the title "Cradle of a Healthy Life: The First Three Years": to look at this seed that has already everything in it, but then needs a whole lifetime to completely unfold.

In the moment of birth, the physical body has already been fashioned. It has already been created over the past nine months. So in a way there has already been a birth of the physical body, but in the beginning it was invisible. The physical body has been already present as a kind of blueprint that will be filled in with matter. In the very beginning there is already a plan that is taken by our self, our individuality, and then filled out, developed, created.

What you see in embryology is that what is finished first—not in all its forms, but in its concept that is already physical—is the head organization. The head, the nervous system, is what is there first. It is not yet formed with eyes and ears and so on, but it is there as a principle, the head principle.

And then there comes this incredible moment when out of the periphery blood cells move in and start to pulsate, when there is no heart yet. And out of the blood cells there forms a heart that is very primitive in the beginning, and the periphery and the center start to pulsate in a kind of conversation. It's not that there is an organ like the liver that is formed like a bud, it's the heart that is formed first. It's actually not in the body yet, it's in front of this developing embryo. And then when the heart starts to beat, when it starts to be an organ, the other organs start to form. So it's the heart that gives the impulse for all the rest of the organs to form.

And when the organs have started to form, only then the extremities, the legs and arms, are initiated. And they are initiated like a new formation. They are not pushed out of this developing small body. They are actually formed out of the periphery. It starts with the hands. It's not that the embryo grows arms and then the hands are formed; it starts with hands and feet, and then they initiate the rest of the arms and the legs.

I don't want to go too deeply into embryology, but just enough that you already see that the head principle is something that from the beginning we already know how to do. Then there come the organs like a gift, a gift from the universe. And then a new creation, our limbs. So you see in embryology already that our limbs come from the future; they do not come from the past. The head comes from the past; the limbs come from the future.

When the first trimester is over, everything is there as a possibility; the rest of the pregnancy is there to build it, to make it more and more complete. So the inner birth of the physical body is at conception, and then it is birthed into the outside, visible world with the moment of birth.

Now today, everything is a little bit different because we cannot wait. What was supposed to be in warm darkness, today we have to look at, give it a name and a gender. This shows our personal freedom—I don't say it is right or wrong—but there is a loss of this gift that I can give my child: to fashion a space without me already prodding in. This is a theme for the first years of life in general.

So the child is born, this unbelievable moment when a mature soul takes on a small body again—I don't think we can give enough feeling to what is happening, that again a soul is taking on a small body. The reason why we do not remember that is that we would not be able to endure it. There are very few people who have a memory all the way back to the moment of birth or even conception. Moving into that small body lets us fall asleep, lets us lose consciousness right away. Because now, something has to happen that we could not make happen if we were conscious. If learning to talk, to walk and to think would be in our freedom, in our conscious choice, can you imagine how we would walk around?

So in taking hold of the body and building into the body the Word—because that's what it's about—in the first days and weeks and months and years of life, it's not about pressing something from the inside out, but meeting the world and building the world into the body. And that is only possible because this is love—complete love, unconditional love in action. Some children cannot give this unconditional love, for whatever reason, and then there are moments when they cannot take the world into their organs. What we call imitation is actually an immediate meeting of our love forces, which are will forces, warmth forces, which flow out as this young being meets the world. It's really immediate: we take this world and we build it into our muscular and nervous system. That is what I have been reading about in the research that I have looked at the past few days.

I was so touched by this research into speech development: that even at two days old, the child dances with the speech of his environment, regardless of whether it is English, Chinese, German, Dutch, Spanish, Japanese. The researchers made videos, and what they wanted to see was how in speech development—that's a little later, in the second year of life—how every consonant, every vowel is accompanied by the movement body of the child. This movement is not just of one muscle; the muscular system is like a sounding board, it's like a musical instrument. And while they were doing this research, and doing hours and hours of video, what they found in the very young child was that this happened not only when the child "sounded" him- or herself, but also when the child listened. And this response to the environment, to the speaking or sounding environment, was so immediate that there was no consciousness in between. It was a "dancing together"—that's what the researcher called it—in the speech world, in the sounding world around. Isn't that unbelievable?[1]

> *An audience member said: That's eurythmy!*

---

[1] This research is found in *Childhood Falls Silent* by Rainer Patzlaff (available from WECAN).

It's eurythmy! It's absolutely eurythmy. So I would like to stop here for a moment, and what I hoped for was that you would share ideas, memories, or pictures out of your own life or those of your children, or out of your classroom. Then what we weave together will be more and more full, and not just a lecture.

> Audience members spoke about:
>
> Experiencing a newborn granddaughter "dancing" up to her mama.
>
> Experiencing with a newborn grandchild how important the singing of lullabies was, how she would settle right down when she heard them.
>
> A comment that Joseph Chilton Pearce said that this movement response to sound begins in utero: the "mother tongue" starts with hearing the mother's voice before birth. She remembered a time when her infant son was crying, and she sang him a song she had sung him before birth, and he stopped crying and she knew that he recognized who she was and responded.
>
> Another spoke of how when she was giving birth, the midwives were not even in the room, because she was not making the kind of sounds normally associated with labor. Her husband said that she was "singing." When her son was born and the midwives asked her for his name, she said the name that had "come" to her before his birth, and on hearing it he smiled (and did not smile again for months).
>
> A story of giving birth to a second set of twins and ending up in a hospital with much noise of beepers and so forth. When the babies' older sisters would come into the room the newborns would immediately respond to their voices, in the midst of all the other noises.

Thank you for saying that, because what this video showed was that noises were not imitated. No noises were imitated, only the human voice. We don't have to be afraid that the beepers will be part of their muscular system, luckily.

> Another comment:
>
> An experience in working with infant and toddler classes: amazement that the very smallest children respond to each other's sounds, whether to happy noises or crying. Seeing that they are "social creatures" from the beginning.

Cradle of a Healthy Life: The First Three Years

You know, in the book *The Challenge of the Will* by Margaret Meyerkort and Rudi Lissau, they call imitation *empathy*. I think this is so right. It's really a force of love, to flow into this world and dance with it. In the little book *The Spiritual Guidance of the Individual and Humanity*, Rudolf Steiner says that for the first two-and-a-half to three years, learning to walk, talk, and think is under the guidance of the loving spirit of our time, the Christ himself. I brought this to my students a week ago and we were talking about that: what does that mean? When you go into how deep this empathy toward the world must be, then you get an inkling of what he meant. This was not meant as religion, because the young child is religion.

So learning to walk, learning to be upright, to conquer space, is the first task young children master. And while they are putting the speech around them into their system, they still have to first master space. That is done with lots of joy, actually. There are some painful things, but learning to walk is done with lots of joy, and a never-ending, never-tiring wish to practice with their movement body.

This ability to walk, to be upright, is guided from the head down. When you look at the very young just-born child, you see that beautifully formed head and that somewhat pitiful—in the sense of arousing compassion—phenomenon of limbs being all over the place, not being able to be coordinated. And so this movement, being able to walk, is guided from the head down; but the head is still asleep, luckily. If you would imagine that we would have to consciously learn the functions of the muscles, the ones that are bending and stretching on the one side or the other—imagine that the head would be conscious of doing that; we would never, ever get to walk. So the head is compassionately put away, and the periphery is awake.

But the head forces are calming, ordering, harmonizing forces, and that's what we need. So while the head is woken up from the periphery in, while the limbs are awake, it's always a kind of conversation between above and below, between calming, ordering, harmonizing forces from above, and these alive, willful, always-fresh, always-wanting-to-practice forces from below.

You can observe how it starts with the eyes, and it moves down the neck, down the back. Then the hands are there, then it goes to the pelvis, the child is able to turn over, to sit, and then to turn around and crawl; and while they are doing these movements, they are practicing with their whole movement body. When you observe this process, you understand that as much as the child needs to be close to the parent—because the closeness brings a sense of security by bringing a proper sense of touch—just as much does the child need to be by him- or herself and practicing with this movement body.

There is often a passionate for-and-against in this area, "attachment parenting" or the opposite, but if you use common sense, the child gives the lead. You put her down and she enjoys it, and then she needs to be with you again. The children give you the cues, and if you can listen to them, then it's not either/or.

The problem is that we are not asleep in our head, and we have all our ideas and judgments and have read a lot and have new fads; so what is asked of us as adults is that we have common sense. This common sense is cued into the child's need, and then there is no right or wrong. Every child needs something a little bit different. There is not one child who needs exactly the same thing as the other. So we don't have to fight, because we have different children, and so if we are cued into them and honest with ourselves, nothing bad should happen. And if we make mistakes the children are actually quite forgiving.

So when this movement has moved down all the way to the tips of the toes, then this is the first maturing, so to speak, and the child is able to stand up. There is the joy of being able to stand up and move toward what you want to touch for all this time. This is the first conscious sense of freedom, to be able to move where you wanted to move and get what you wanted to get. If you have children, you remember how fast they can get to where they wanted to get.

And then this whole process is repeated, because now the child has to move deeper into the movement body and make it supple. In the beginning it is quite stiff. In the beginning when a child walks, you can see that his center of movement is actually far above him. The feet are not yet moved from inside the body, but from outside of the body. You can actually see how in the next seven years, the center of movement slowly moves into the child. When he has again, for the second time, reached the tips of his toes he is able to jump rope, to overcome gravity.

Overcoming gravity is a sign of how our highest principle, which we call our ego—which is not conscious yet in having goals or intentions for life, that is still working completely in the body—how this ego, this incarnated ego, moves all the way through and deals immediately with gravity, overcoming gravity. Then we can lift ourselves up.

Then you will see that for the second time, now, the soul/spirit has moved through the body. It will do it over and over and over again. Then when you get into your sixties you can actually feel how you are moving in and out at the same time. You can hold your center and be totally in the periphery, which when you are 45 or even 50 you are not able to do yet. That's the gift of getting older.

When you watch children and observe when they are able to climb the stairs, when they are able to go down the stairs, when they are able to turn around and look at something that is behind them, these are all steps in a conscious development of learning to walk, which we take for granted. But these are big steps, and so is the joy that comes with them.

When they are able to turn around, when they are able to be not so stiff in their own body, at about two-and-a-half or three years, they start to be able to recognize their social environment and to take in the other children through a freed chest region. If you look at a one-year-old or a two-year-old looking at another child, and then at a three-and-a-half or four-year-old, and look again at their companions in the classroom, that's a totally different kind of meeting.

So now comes something that might change your classroom when you go back. In the first three years, the children—let me say the soul/spirits—go into the world selflessly imitating. And they do that with a sense of touch that we actually cannot completely fathom. The sense of touch for very young children is not only that they touch a surface and realize that here is a surface and here I am, which is important—but while young children touch the surface, they realize the wholeness, the whole form of what they touch.

So when you take the ball, and when you touch the ball, you can take it and feel that it's a rubber ball, it's smooth, you have to move around a little bit. But the child will touch that ball and through this completely unadulterated sense of wholeness be able to perceive the whole ball as a totality, which we as adults have a hard time with. We can think it, but we have a hard time to feel it at the same time. Sometimes when we are in an almost altered state, when we are in love or have had an incredibly wonderful experience, then we touch something and we can feel the whole thing suddenly. Then we lose it again because our thinking is making a separation between what we perceive and the mental picture, the concept that we make of it. We perceive, and then we have a concept, so this moment of touching and getting the wholeness is for us a split second and then it's gone.

For young children, because they do not separate yet, they do not make concepts yet, the concept is still experience. Can you imagine how the world is when you touch, and always out of what you touch something whole appears? And now imagine that you put around the child things that are not true, so that the sense of touch and the object that originates out of the sense of touch are actually not congruent. Take a plastic block: you take the block and it looks heavy and big, and then your experience of this thing is light. You get an experience of the world that is not true, because an object that is so big is actually supposed to be heavy.

Or when you give only square forms—there are no square forms in nature in this world. If the child always touches something that is not found in nature there is a separation between the experienced perception and the truth of the object. And you imbue into the children a sense of anxiety because when they flow into the world with this incredible trust and love, they expect that the world is good and true. And then when they touch a world that doesn't match, there is anxiety injected into the child's future thinking. In these early years it is not thinking yet, it is perception-experience. Perception is immediately experience.

So if the environment of the child is not true, if what he touches is not true, we are not only infiltrating him with anxiety, but also with doubt. And with this doubt there come children who are cynical, because their expectations are not met. How can you survive this sense of betrayal—because it is a sense of betrayal? By saying "I don't care."

Can you see how these very early days and weeks and months are important, not only for learning to walk, but also for later life? They build a sense of trust.

Then we go a little bit further. If that which I perceive and that which I experience are congruent, later when I learn to think, that which I perceive and the concept I build of it will also be congruent. And this type of thinking is necessary for a thinking that is able to freely experience the world each time anew again.

When you observe children's thinking, they are able to do something we do not do any more as adults. It's a kind of relational thinking: they are able to connect everything they perceive with everything else. And there come these incredible ideas about how the moon and the mother and the dog and the father are all fitting together—and we smile, and we write them down. It's an incredibly creative kind of thinking. Where does this come from? Their ability to connect, to make relationships between the different perceptions of the world, is so alive.

We lose that as we grow up. A young person of fourteen is in a different place, because the fourteen-year-old knows exactly what is right or wrong. This is how it is and they know, and then they argue. That is when thinking has to become for the first time most physical. For young children thinking is not physical at all; they still think in the etheric world. It's crucial for the way we are later as adults. When we are in our sixties and we are not able to understand younger people anymore because we cannot wrap our thoughts around what another person says, that is when they get fixed. And the origins lie in early life, in the materials of the kindergarten. I really mean it: the *materials* of your kindergartens.

The young child is incredibly matter-of-fact. She doesn't say "Oh, what a beautiful flower," but "How can I smell the flower, or touch the flower; how is it when I carry the pot?" The child is a little scientist. Never again in our lives are we so unconditionally open to the sciences as is a young child.

I want to make the next step: what you do as an adult in the kindergarten, or in the nursery, the preschool, or even younger, has an effect on the children: an effect on what kind of experiential concepts or perceptions—I have to put these things together because they are not separated yet—are built into their body, their thought body. So for the children it is important that they see you do everyday things. The younger the children, the more important it is that they see you sweep, and cut, and cook, and clean, and do things they will find later in the world. It's not about what you think is "nice." That will not help the children to get a full picture of the world, because if what you think is nice is not what they experience in a full touching way, they will not be able to put it into their experiential body.

This might change your way of working in your kindergarten, because it is so important that the children observe you doing meaningful things.

I will stop here again, if you have comments.

> *A participant spoke about the common misperception about what it means to meet children's needs: "You need to eat an apple, so I'm going to cut it up and give it to you." What they need is actually the whole picture.*

Right. They need to see the whole process; it's not just being fed with an apple. That makes the will lazy.

> *More comments:*

The angels only experience the physical world through how we interact with it; it seems as though it's the same for children, coming from the angelic world. So if our interactions are loving and practical it seems true to them, it feeds them.

The young child as a scientist: a characterization by Eugene Schwartz, of the young child in the garden being able to pick a strawberry that had been ripened by the sun… versus the grocery store strawberry from California… versus the strawberry-shaped eraser that comes as a party favor. The ether body starts to step back each time.

About touching and feeling the wholeness: a 16-month-old went up to a little girl and started licking her face; he just wanted to taste her! Another time, he met a younger child and first touched her gently but then just had to grab her, needing to feel the wholeness.

A memory of a participant's own childhood, feeling how when adults were not there for her in thought, there was a separation. This led to a resolve in adulthood that when a child approached her she would have her thoughts present.

The children are connected with each other and with us directly, immediately, in the etheric realm. To the extent that they are not awake in their thinking forces, they are experiencing our thoughts and feelings. And so they actually feel our feelings. This is not conscious, but they build it into their organs.

This could make us afraid to be around young children. The human being is so plastic, so forgiving as a wholeness…but some of our illnesses in later life have to do with that we took up some of the feelings of our mother and father. If we didn't take destiny and karma into consideration, we could feel betrayed and victimized by this: "Why didn't they…" But if you realize that even in these very early days and weeks, you are the one who initiated to be with this person, with this family. And what you live out in your physical body, in your organs, carries karma. Karma lives in our physical body, not in our intentions. If it were left to our intentions, we would never go to where we need to go to experience pain. But in the physical body we have imprinted the laws of our own karma, so that what happens in early life, and will bear out in later life, has to do with our own decision. When I realized that it was such a sense of relief, because I didn't want to be a victim. I wanted to be the maker of my own karma.

I was born after the war in Germany, and though I didn't hear any planes or any sirens, my parents and my Oma carried that around in their own ether body, and so I was part of it. I dreamt the dreams of my family, which was not very pleasant. But through that, I deeply understand why war is not an option. It's in my body. So we must trust in the choices of our children, even if they are painful ones, even as we have the utmost responsibility for what we put around them.

The pre-requisite for thinking is this imitating-perceiving, this empathetic meeting of the world that is built into our organ systems, so that it lives in our liver, our kidneys, our lungs, and our heart. What *moves* around us is built into our muscular systems, what *lives* around us into our organs. And so when Rudolf Steiner was asked, "How can we help the young child to be healthy?" he said that common sense, joy, and laughter are the best forces to breed healthy organs. He didn't say anthroposophy, meditation, and so on. That's for you. But for the young child it's common sense, joy, and laughter. We can do that!

With my colleagues now, we are studying Rudolf Steiner's "Self-Education through Spiritual Science," and we were very surprised to find in this lecture that self-education comes through meeting the world. Not by sitting, but by meeting the world and becoming conscious of it. And we said: this is what the child does through play. Children are self-educating when they are playing, and at different ages they play differently. A toddler is not so interested in toys, but she opens the cupboards and drawers and puts things in and out and spills this and that. That is their play, their scientific play.

Later, in the middle years of early childhood, they play their experiences throughout the day. And this play is sacred, because we actually do not know what play is. Too many times we try to initiate play that has to do with our world, not with their world. And so this needs to revolutionize our kindergartens, too: that deep trust that whatever the children play in these years is the best they can work with at that time.

Renate Long-Breipohl in Australia brought a book to the International Conference in Wilton last year that is not yet translated: *Spiel aus der Tiefe*, which means "play out of the depths," by Maria Luisa Nuesch. There's a kindergarten teacher in Switzerland who works in the most horrendous part of cities, where children are malnourished and mistreated. And then she describes how the children work through their inner "stuff" and she is just present. She describes situations where I don't think we would be able to let it happen, because it looks so destructive. And then she describes this process, that the child heals his own trauma by being allowed to go through the process…as long as an adult is present and he can feel he is safe. He can go into these bad places because there is someone around who holds the space.

Some things we cannot do in our kindergartens, because it is disturbing for other children, so we have to find the balance. But she said that even if a child runs around in circles for some time, we have to trust that this is how she or he works out something that happened.

There are more and more boys who do not want to fit into the "nice" Waldorf kindergarten. We have to ask ourselves how we can help. Is there enough work around? Because they go home and mother and father work at the computer; they do not see real work done any more. And then they should be part of the circle, but what they want to do is real work. I think we have the material to make our kindergartens ready for all children who come.

The reason is not only to get the children calm, but also because this working out of inner trauma will result in a healthy later life. If it is not worked out in the moment, or in this time where it will be built into the organs, it will work on the liver. It will work on the sense of self, and then we have children who later are violent or angry.

So this feeling for the etheric life in your kindergarten, this more and more conscious understanding for what is etherically in your kindergarten is not only about rhythm. Rhythm is important and wonderful, but the etheric also lives in how your children learn to think and to express themselves. This needs to be more and more an experience for us as educators too.

In *Childhood Falls Silent,* a report by Rainer Patzlaff, who has written extensively about media in early childhood, we find that not only is illiteracy spreading throughout the world, but there is less and less of the spoken word. Research done in the 1990s in Germany showed that the spoken word in families was down to two-word sentences: "Hurry up," "What do you want," "Put on your shoes." And it was down to binary responses from the children: yes and no. Not full sentences any more. And so "childhood falls silent": children not only don't want to read, but they don't want to speak any more. At the time of this research, every fifth child had speech pathology. And I see it more and more now in the kindergartens children who need to go to specialists. It has to do with not enough spoken word around to lovingly imitate. With a verse like "nibble, nibble little mouse," the repetition of sounds like N and F and B is pure joy to the children, even when it doesn't mean very much to us.

That doesn't mean that parents should now go and say "nibble nibble…" but that the children need to speak their language, love it and speak it. It's not only about reading stories, but also how we talk to each other. In England, they had a program for six-year-olds to help them learn how to ask for directions, or other things, because they came to first grade without any capacity to get around in the world. How do we learn to speak? How can we support it, and what are the hindrances? These are the questions for us today.

The First Three Years
PART II

As early childhood teachers, you have lots and lots of forces of imagination. Now I need you to imagine that I'm drawing on the blackboard and you see what I'm drawing.

I do not want to introduce new concepts to you, but I want to work a little bit with the very important partner of the child: that is, you. In order to help the child to freedom, you need to know about yourself. There is no way around it, you cannot fake it or avoid it: you have to look at yourself and you have to work with yourself.

In what is around you, in your aura, you carry the realness of yourself. That's where we actually become more and more afraid or doubtful, because there are so many forces that want to pull us in one direction or the other, either into doubt or fear. It is very hard to find the middle ground. In order to look at that a little bit, I would like to look at how the development of the child is mirrored in the different ages through adulthood.

So on this imaginary blackboard, I will make a U-form. On the left side there is a 0, then a 7, then comes 14, 21 at the bottom, then 28, 35, and 42. And then you see that if you make a line through the points right and left on this U-form, you connect the 0 and 42, 7 and 35, 14 and 28.

I want you to see a straight line underneath the U-form. The times on that start with negative-8 months, then it goes to 0, then 3, then 7, then 10, then 14, then 21.

So I would like to start with this straight line first. Eight months before birth is what we could call the inner birth of the physical body. This is not my invention; it comes from the wonderful book *The First Seven Years* by Edmund Schoorel, a school doctor in Holland.

Then at the point of birth, there is the outer birth of the physical body and the inner birth of the ether body, the life body. The inner birth of the life body means that now this newly born body is able to maintain its life forces. Heartbeat, breathing, warmth—it's still very tender, but it's there. So we have the outer birth of the physical body and the inner birth of the ether body.

At three years of age, when through the help of the hierarchies the child has learned to be upright, to speak, and to think, there comes a time when the soul rocks a little bit because on a deep unconscious level the child feels that these higher powers recede a little bit, to let the child go into freedom. This is the time of the "terrible twos," of temper tantrums. This is the inner birth of the astral body. If we are in touch with our feeling body, we become ever so dimly aware of our effect on the outside world. The child starts to feel, "What I do has an effect"—it's not given up to the surrounding any more. So this is the inner birth of the astral body, which will have its outer birth at fourteen.

At seven is the outer birth of the etheric, the time of the change of teeth.

At ten, this time of the so-called nine/ten-year change, when again the soul rocks, it's the inner birth of the ego, where the child now feels "I'm alone, I'm different, I'm out of paradise." This ego organization will be born at twenty-one.

So to repeat again, and see it with your inner eye:

Eight months before birth: Inner birth of the physical body

Birth: Outer birth of the physical body, inner birth of the etheric body

Three: Inner birth of the astral body

Seven: Outer birth of the etheric body

Ten: Inner birth of the ego

Fourteen: Outer birth of the astral body

Twenty-one: Outer birth of the ego

We see that the tension between the inner and the outer birth is getting greater and greater. In order to come to a proper outer birth of our members, physical body, etheric body, astral body and ego, we need a lot of time to practice. The higher our members are, the more time we need to practice. So at twenty-one, when a young person is conscious of "this is what I want to do in life"—we go now to the U-form—the ego turns back on itself and works on its soul qualities. And from twenty-one to twenty-eight, the ego works through the astral body to create the sentient, the feeling soul. This is when young people are so full of ideas and so social, as never again in life. If they are healthy, they love life, the world, other people. The way they can be with one another is really exemplary for all of us. That's the feeling soul.

Then from twenty-eight to thirty-five, we get a bit cool. That's the time when the ego works through the etheric body to create a kind of two-fold member. One is more connected to the heart forces, to the feeling; the other to the mind forces, the intellect. That is what we could call the intellectual or mind soul, or you could say the heart-and-mind soul. This already has a distance from the world, not flowing out into the world any more like a young child.

Then between thirty-five and forty-two, we acquire something that is called the consciousness soul. The consciousness soul is what the ego works out of the physical body. And now go back to what we talked about this morning: how important it is that the child has an environment that is real, that the child brings into his body the reality of people and the world. If that has happened properly, the consciousness soul is free to hold diverse opinions and not get caught in "this is right, this is wrong." This does not belong any more after the thirty-fifth year of life.

So at forty-two, our consciousness soul is the first vessel that can hold spirit in itself without being connected to the body. It can look at things from all sides, can hold many different opinions and let them be. So our self, our true self, which is of a spiritual nature, is only free when we are forty-two.

If you are older than forty-two, you can look back on your own biography. I in my sixties can feel this, that when I am so attached to my own opinion and cannot let go of it, I feel it in my body. Because I am *right*. That is not the consciousness soul. The consciousness soul can let go of it and look at it from a different place; that is freedom. This is only possible if in the physical body—which is not the matter body alone—there is the truthfulness of the first three years established.[1]

---

1 For more on the stages of development, see *The Human Life* by George and Gisela O'Neil.

So in our teacher training we work with the early childhood and the grades on healing your own biography by going into these early years and finding out where you got stuck. Because if you know where you got stuck you can work on it and the children don't have to push your buttons all the time.

I work with that in medicine, too—it is the ego working out of the bodily sheaths on a soul level from twenty-one to forty-two. Things appear on a soul level that have to be anchored in the physical level. Sometimes there are incredible correlations.

When we are born, we inherit a body from our parents. Genes are real! It's not that in anthroposophy there are no genes. We have an inherited body that comes from our ancestors, but we inherit it to overcome it and make it into our own. That is the drama of the first seven years. The child tries to take this inherited body as a model body, but then at seven he has his own. If that is not possible, sometimes you have to work through things in your thirties and forties, but in these first seven years it happens organically. And the helpers in this process of overcoming the inherited body are illnesses. So that's why we want to have some illnesses, not because it's so nice to have a fever, but because the fever burns the inherited body through.

You have to be careful, because some illnesses are destructive. That's not what we want. We want to support the child in burning through a body that is resisting. The body doesn't fit properly. Sometimes it seems to fit really nicely, but for most children it doesn't. Some of the behavior problems in the kindergarten have to do with this, that the body doesn't fit properly. And so they flail and scream, and the interesting thing is that the children who scream are the ones who are strong enough to try to get through. We have to worry about the ones who are completely compliant. If they feel so comfortable in their bodies it's much harder to get to their own individuality.

The whole of Waldorf education is about educating toward freedom. We want to see the child feeling free: "This is my instrument, it sounds like me, not my mother and father." So that's why they try to work it through. And it starts very early. When they have these horrible colics and screaming for hours, Steiner says the same forces that the children scream with, trying to make their bodies fit, are forces that when understood and guided properly are forces of morality. With the same vigor, the same verve, they can later strive to be there for morality. So imagine that you dampen them down all the time, say "That's not okay, that's wrong." Today we tranquilize our children from very early on, and that is actually a message: "You are wrong, your spirit is wrong, your body is right." So many children give up.

Don't be afraid of your loud ones. Be happy about your loud ones. It's not that they need to scream your kindergarten down—they need to be guided—but there is a lot of raw material to be guided.

Is there anyone who wants to share?

> *Would an accident be included? At age six the participant was always way behind everyone, then she fell and broke her arm. From that moment she was always ahead.*

That's right. If children today cannot get the childhood illnesses they look for other things and they have an accident. Accidents go deep into the etheric body.

> *Question: If a child is not able to overcome the body before age seven, that will manifest later in life?*

All our lives. We are amazing people; we can change until we die.

> *Continuation of question: Can the same illnesses that cropped up then unresolved, crop up again?*

In a different form, yes. It gets deeper and more severe. You all know about the transforming power of illness; you always have to weigh whether it is destructive, but even then, you can die of cancer and be healed. A strange concept, but it's true.

> *Comment on receiving anxiety as a child through materials that are not true: As we get older, it seems like we play it over again. We go out from college into the world with big dreams and we find the "box" we think will be heavy but it's actually light.*

That's right! Throughout our life we always find the boxes that are meant to be heavy and are actually light—or the other way around—and in adult life there are many "betrayals" like that.

> *A question about children who are reluctant to lose teeth. What is the relationship between that and the etheric?*

It's not just the losing of teeth, it's when the child is able to form for herself a second set that is her own. If a child is not able to build the second teeth and push them through, there is this hesitancy of the etheric body to come free for learning. There is no pat answer; you have to look at what to do, whether to hold them back another year or something else. Teething today is so individual. I would still not pull them, even if there is a second set waiting. I would help with homeopathy, or therapeutic eurythmy can get them to come out very quickly.

> *More about teeth: a child has the second teeth coming without losing the first. He won't stop crying and she doesn't know what to do.*

All of these transitions, where you have to let go of something and go to the next, are accompanied by anxiety. Some children want to turn back, because they are anxious. They feel "If I lose my teeth, I will have to go on to the next step and I don't want to." So they hold onto them. They need a lot of affirmation, not through your words, but through your thoughts, working with the senses. You can work a lot with the sense of touch, establishing a feeling of trust. This child needs help. Crying means he is actually "out," he is too sensitive out here, and crying pulls him back in. So he needs to be helped to pull himself back in, through cuddling. *This child doesn't want to be held.* That doesn't mean he doesn't need it. You can work with baths, or with brushing, if he doesn't want to be held.

> *A question about a child whose teeth are not coming through. A dentist says he sees this more and more: molars not forming when he x-rays to look for them.*

It makes perfect sense today; the child's life body is so overburdened with too many sense impressions—if it's not an inherited weakness. The teeth today are so individual, because there is so much the children have to work with. It is literally the ether body that builds them and pushes them out.

> *So he just can't do it, he is overwhelmed?*

I don't know, I would have to see him, but that would be a concern.

Now I would like to go further. Our life does not end at forty-two; and now you have to imagine on the blackboard a larger U-form. Now it has thirty-five as its lowest point. Now if you continue in seven-year steps, you will come all the way to sixty-three. So this lower part, the stages before and after thirty-five, is the part where we are under the influence of the Sun. On the one hand we are standing in the light of the Sun, which is the most social of our planetary bodies: the sun shines on everything, without leaving anything out. It has no bias. And while we are in the inner light of the sun, outwardly we are in our darkest place.

While we develop our consciousness soul, we are the most deeply connected to our body. We are the most material. At thirty-five, our body goes down, and now what has been given to us, what happens more or less by itself, is not enough any more. Now we have to work on ourselves so as not to go down with our body. And if you are over thirty-five, go back to that time and remember what a dark time it was. On the one hand, you are discouraged, or disappointed by your life until then; your enthusiasm has left you somewhat; you are in the dark woods, so to speak. And then in this time of being most connected to the body, rightfully so, one realizes, "If I am not finding my own way, I will go down." It's an inner experience of dying.

And then in this experience of dying comes our second moon node: thirty-six and a few months. It is full of wisdom that it comes at that time, because the whole array of constellations in the universe at the moment of our birth are imprinted into the finer structures of our brain. It's like a map, our life map. That's what true astrology is about: we have a map in our brain, which our higher, inner being looks all the time because it's like a road map for our life. Then we go astray, and there comes for the first time the moon node—the sun, moon and earth are at the same position as when we are born. That comes at eighteen years and six months. Then our inner being knocks and says "What about…?" Then we are reminded. There are things that are more individual, and things that are more social karma.

This comes again when we are around thirty-six or thirty-seven. Then it knocks a little stronger, and that's when if we cannot listen we get sick or have an accident. That will happen again eighteen years later when we are fifty-six. Then it is very urgent. If we have gone astray, fifty-six is a very difficult time in many lives. Many people get cancer, heart disease, depression, anxieties, fears.

All this is less traumatic if you had the luck to have parents and caregivers who helped you, already in your first seven years of life, to come to ever-so-dim inner understanding of what your life is supposed to be. This is not conscious. But it's not that our karma starts when we are fourteen; it's already in our body when we're much younger, only when we're fourteen we become conscious of it. But it's there before.

And if we can help as parents and caregivers to remove hindrances—that's what education is about—if we can help to remove hindrances, then life doesn't have to be so traumatic.

So I have to go back to how we can help children to live their own lives.

First of all that we let them work on their own instrument, on their own body, in a way that is helpful, is healthy; and secondly what I said this morning: that we take play in the kindergarten really seriously. Play in the kindergarten is the helper for health. We try to impose our adult understanding of the world onto the children who come with a new script. We are old; they have a new script. They know what they want to find, and we put our own concepts on them. You see how we already start to deviate.

So as people of the kindergarten we need to be rhythmical, worthy of imitation. As adults, thinking about what is right for the children, we have to be revolutionaries, not take something and do it because it has been done forever like that. I'm not saying that you have to change your kindergarten every week because you are revolutionary. Together with your faculty you find ways that are new and meet the child of the twenty-first century. Since we do have this doubt and we are not quite healthy any more — I don't think any one of us is—we need the faculty, or we need our assistants, or our husbands or our friends, to bounce ideas back and forth and by exchanging ideas come to a new level of understanding.

And the third thing is to know about child development. This is paramount. That's why Waldorf education is not only that you have nice materials—you can do that easily—but that you more and more understand child development in its width and breadth.

And so a student of mine said "How often have I heard you talk about the first three years and it's never boring?" You can go over it again and again and it's always new. And that's what we need to do. Have we understood it? That we are sitting here together is really wonderful.

I will here stop again for questions and then we will finish up for today. Is there anything about this course of life?

> *Where is the most courage needed for early childhood teachers?*

If you go to the end of *Study of Man*, it says, "Have courage for the truth." So, to have the courage to look at the truth of the situation, of the child today, of your kindergarten: does it meet the child in your kindergarten? Do you do your circle because you love this circle and it belongs to the season, or does it meet your children? Sometimes you need to continue with the circle and stop doubting. We all know, as adults we doubt all the time. If the children do not imitate right away then we think there is something wrong with us. But we must have this courage for the truth: "Am I real in what I'm doing? Am I really in the circle? Am I so strong that I really believe it, or do I just noodle it along?" The children force us to be courageous for the truth.

And then there comes something we need to re-imagine, like play. We have not taken play seriously enough to really work on it, investigate it, talk with each other, ask, "What does that mean?" Then we have to be courageous enough to implement what we find out. Maybe my nice inside classroom needs to be outside for half of the time. Maybe I have to get rid of some of the dolls because they do not help. Maybe I have to get rid of some of the "nice" toys. I love them, but the children don't really. This kind of courage is what we need.

> *A participant told about a boy who talks incessantly. She realized at the home visit that he has two teenage sisters and intellectual parents who don't know why it's important to play and don't know how. She asked them to sit on the floor with him and see what happened; he started to play more.*

It's actually not true that the children of today do not imitate any more. The forces from the head are the ones that calm, cool, order, but they inhibit the will coming from below. So you have to get stronger in what you put out to be imitated. Then the children, even if they do not show that they imitate, they cannot help but imitate. Then slowly, you will push back the forces from the head and they will imitate again, even if they are "cool." When you really observe them, you will see that they do imitate. It's not so easy anymore because the head forces are so strong, but there's lots of hope.

> *A request for more about how at sixty-three or sixty-four you can be in and out at the same time*

When you look at the mirroring, at a newborn child from birth to three and the older person from sixty to sixty-three—this is not something I read, but something that came to me, that I could feel—as the child has this practical love through empathy and imitation, and by imitating they get the wholeness of the world, I start to feel that I can now wrap my soul around things and feel them, but consciously, lovingly, without having to judge, because I am a little bit out of my body. I can feel it and do it at the same time, where the child does it but is not conscious of it yet. It's conscious love now, conscious practical love.

I want to go back a little bit. It's interesting to look at us adults, but it's important that you as early childhood educators have the whole of childhood in your imagination, because you want to imagine where the children will be when they are twenty-one. Not that you do it all the time, but it's important to know where they will be. The picture that I think can be pretty exact is that when you look at the newborn child, everything is like a bud. It's all inside still. It's like a bud that slowly opens up. Then when the ten-year change comes, this bud breaks open and the flower is visible. The petals are visible. Then when the young person is twelve and then fourteen, they break through. They break through their muscles and their bones. Their soul-spiritual being is breaking through. After fourteen they stand in front of you as a different human being, Steiner says, but totally raw. These protective leaves have fallen off and now they are standing in their whole flower, but raw. They are aware of their rawness, and they will try to hide. That's why the boys pull on these hoods, because it is so painful to be exposed and to have a feeling of the soul birth, in such an immediate way.

And at the same time when they are so raw and when they have fallen with their bodily nature into heaviness, they receive a new heart. This heart carries the highest ideals and intentions. So they meet the world with a new heart, a new etheric heart, with which they meet the world with the highest expectations. While before they still could forgive the teachers their inadequacies, when they are fourteen it's not possible any more. They look at their parents, and it's painful to have these parents because they see that these wonderful parents who used to be gods in the beginning and then slowly came down, but at least were nice—now it's painful, and they turn away because they cannot bear it that their parents are so human.

They turn their idealism toward other people: the teacher, or the doctor. When they come into my office I have the easiest time because they tell me everything. And then they look at their parents, and their parents look just like me! I'm not better, but they cannot bear that their parents are so normal.

Then in this time of the rawness—again, it's about truth—comes the truth of the sciences and the truth of the stories in a different way. Through the Parzival story they realize that it's OK to make mistakes, it's OK to feel awkward, it's OK to kill the wrong person. It's OK because in the end, that person who is so awkward will be the Grail King. In ninth grade, it's when it's the most difficult especially for the boys, because sometimes they look as if they have no will left, as if they are zombies. When you fold yourself into yourself, when you let yourself fall into yourself, you don't expose yourself so completely. It's almost a physical feeling of rawness. And then in tenth grade it gets better, but then comes a new feeling of despair. It's still the birth of the astral body, where right and wrong, deep despair and great happiness, rule. Then in this time there comes *Hamlet*. "I have two souls within my chest."[2] Hamlet makes mistakes too: there are lots of dead people at the end on the stage.

Sometimes we think that Waldorf education is for early childhood, and we give a good foundation and then we can let our children grow up; but actually Waldorf education is possible until they are in twelfth grade. The curriculum still meets their inner development in an incredible way. It's not just another nice story.

All that I have talked about, from the beginning of life up to twenty-one and then from twenty-one all the way to sixty-three, is about the path to freedom, which has to do with our body. Only in our body, only in the physical body can we develop freedom—which is a mystery in itself. Why do we need a body to be able to develop freedom? But that would be another conference.

---

2 This quotation is not found in Shakespeare's *Hamlet*, but in Goethe's *Faust*. However, Rudolf Steiner speaks of Hamlet as a student of Faust ; see for example *Old and New Methods of Initiation*, Lecture 11 (Dornach, February 24, 1922).

The First Three Years
PART III

In olden times when you passed a sage, you didn't know that the person was wise, because he or she was so simple. You would say, "That's a sage? That's a wise person?" because their advice was so simple. And that's what you as early childhood people are—not simpletons, but very simple and real. That's what the children need, not complicated things. Today I will speak about thinking, which is always a little hard—because how can we recognize and foster thinking in our children? This is so important because hardly anybody can think today. We "think," but we cannot *think*. Thinking needs will; it needs will to really think.

In the Winter 2008 research bulletin from the Waldorf Research Institute there is the most wonderful article called "Thinking and the Consciousness of the Young Child," by Renate Long-Breipohl, down in Australia. If you find anything by Renate always grab it because she is one of the early childhood teachers who also trained academically; she studied religious philosophy. She was very much in the thinking process before she became a Waldorf teacher, and as a Waldorf teacher she could heal the one-sidedness of the thinking without losing the ability of thinking herself. So she is a wonderful resource when you want to find something written by a Waldorf educator in very clear thoughts.

As I said yesterday, after venturing out in all the new research done, and being in awe at all the things that are being discovered, when you go back to reading Dr. Steiner, you are amazed that he talked about it already. But he puts it in words such that you have to discover how much is in the sentences. And so if you have the feeling that Steiner is too hard for me, it's too dry, that means that you have to chew it a little harder. Steiner is like good bread, solid bread, without butter and cheese and honey. You just have to chew it until it unfolds its sweetness, because it's inherent. It's very precious. He's actually far ahead of our time, and so if Steiner would disappear out of our reading, it would be such a pity because he helps us to think. Even if you take one sentence in a study group and try to mull it over and over and over again, that in itself is already learning to think.

Let me go back. The children come from the spiritual world. And in the spiritual world, thinking, feeling, and willing are not separate. Thinking is a being and has feeling and will. The thought is a being, has beingness, and has feeling and will in itself. It's a little hard—one has to meditate on that. Thinking as such has beingness.

And then because of being in a body in order to come to freedom, we have to separate out the will of the thought and the feeling of the thought and the thinking, so that we can think without having a feeling right away, and without having to do something right away. That would be a creative power—can you imagine having a thought that comes immediately with the whole wisdom in it? You could not err, you could not make a mistake. That's the consciousness of an angel. The wisdom of the thought in itself is completely there in the moment when the thought is present.

We push the will aside and the feeling aside, and think, so that we can be free—because there needs to be some time before we go into action. It happens the other way around too, but today we want to talk about thinking. So in this moment of being able to push down the feeling and being able not to react right away is the freedom in our thinking. This is not the same for the young child. They come out of the spiritual world, which is a different form of consciousness. They come into a body and still have the freshness that perception immediately has a response, a bodily response. So when the world is perceived by young children, they respond to it immediately by dancing with it or feeling with it. When we talk about the young child as a sense organ, the response to this perception is immediate.

And then in the course of the first three years, this fullness, this wholeness that we have talked about, starts to be separated, so that the feeling content of the perception is touched and practiced by speaking it. When the child speaks the sounds, saying "Bbbbbmmmmm…" they still feel the fullness of the *B* and the *M*, they still actually taste, touch, feel. And then they start to separate a little bit, that this *B* and *M* belong to something that is outside of them. This is the beginning of speaking. So when they start to speak, only then when the sounds have been practiced, a name is given to that which they have been feeling and sensing. That is called naming. That which feels so round, the *B*, becomes a ball. That which feels so warm becomes a bubble, or bubble bath. Only when they can separate from the world a little bit, by naming that which is felt so intensely in the whole body, is the "ball" now out there. In this separation, they have to make a connection between that which is felt and that which is perceived out there. And this connection between me and what is out there, that is thinking for the young child.

The children connect again what they needed to separate. In the beginning, for example with mother's milk, everything is felt, sensed, enjoyed or not enjoyed, all the way down to the tips of the toes. You can observe how this little being actually shudders, feeling the sweetness of the milk all the way to the tiptoes. Being a sense organ means being completely in perception, feeling. When we start to separate the perception, then the first concept comes about. But the concept is still very close. It is felt. And this which is felt is naming, speech. And then when it's separate enough, when the concept and the percept are separate enough, we have to make the connection between the two. That's thinking.

Thinking is the least of our human faculties that we have today. We are so bad at thinking. We have lots of information; we can go to the computer and call up the information; but what is the hardest in teacher training is to think clear thoughts together. It is almost painful to have a thought that is so clear that it can stand by itself. That's why we cannot read Steiner anymore, not because he's so old or dry. We feel that it is dry because in thinking you actually put have to back the feeling content by thinking it clearly. The feeling content and the perception come back, but we have to do it ourselves.

Today there is so much difficulty in the world because when we think something we immediately feel it, and it is selfishly felt. I see it in myself all the time: I listen to the radio, I hear somebody speak, and he says something I cannot bear. I cannot do it. I have to turn it off. But that's a weakness in myself, that I'm not able to listen to a thought or to think a thought from the beginning to the end and then make a decision afterwards, because I'm still so connected to my feelings with it.

It's the same when you hear something you feel good about: the danger of not being able to listen to people and think a thought and then make your decision. I turn on the radio and think, "Oh, it's so great" and again turn it off. I actually do not think. I live in enjoyment and disgust, and then my actions are not informed by a thought process that I have ended, they are informed by my feelings. I haven't even thought it through to the end.

And I assure you that in every conference when we get to thinking there is some resistance. But we have to think clearly as adults for the children to pick it up—the children are also connected to our thought processes. Not only are they connected to the way we move or the way we sing or the way we do things, but they are also connected to our thought processes. So what can we do?

We have to go back and humbly look at the world. What is it, how does it look? Not immediately naming it, but looking at the perception and seeing what concept comes. Describe.

Carl Gustav Jung—such an inspired and inspiring thinker—he writes in his autobiography, that at times in his life he had to humbly go down on his bottom and sit in the sand tray again. And then he was making sand castles and doing what the young child does, observing sand, playing with stones. Can you believe it? So it's not about reading the next difficult book, it's about getting down and sitting in the mud again and observing.

Yesterday we talked about courage for the truth. It means to be humble enough to return to your origins, and realize that you don't know much.

So how can we live around a child, how can we get the courage, knowing all that, to be around the child? And now we need to know that the child, especially the young child from birth to three—that child that we hardly see in the kindergartens yet, but this is the foundation for the children we have in the kindergarten—the very young child cannot help but take in everything around, pleasant or unpleasant. This is this unbelievable selfless love in action, which is called imitation.

And now we need the gift of the night. Because in the night, in sleep, this child's soul will sort out what to keep and what not to keep—luckily. Children will sort out with the help of their guardian angel, which is our higher self, what they want to keep and what not to keep. And what they keep or don't keep goes in accordance to their destiny, to their karma.

Every night when we go to sleep, with the help of our guardian angel or higher self, we actually look over not only our day but our whole life. And every night we actually look back all the way to the beginning: what did we sort out, what did we keep. We look at the pattern of our karma every night. And the first threads, the first patterns are laid in these very early days, weeks, and months of our early, early childhood years, when we are still completely open and cannot help but imitate what is around us.

Now today it is almost a danger that there is not enough to take into the sleep. Because remember, it's not the noises of the day. It's the realness of the environment that is taken into the night. Human voices. Human interactions. Trees. Birds. That is taken into sleep. Even human interactions that are not pleasant. Not the noises of the cars and the computers and so on. So sometimes there is not enough food to weave the tapestry of karma, because the people around do not interact. This is again not something to say "now I know," it's more that one has to put it on and live with it and say "What does that mean?" What is the food for the night? Many, many children today are not able to sleep anymore; there are many sleeping problems for the babies, for the newborns. I see in my practice that children cannot sleep any more. So what does that mean?

So I will stop here for your thoughts, your ideas, your moments of "Oh, now I get it!" that you want to share here.

> *A participant spoke about thinking, feeling and willing being connected: in Waldorf education we don't introduce the abstractness of reading so early. The book* The Alphabet Versus the Goddess *speaks about the relative peacefulness of preliterate cultures.*

Now we are in the twenty-first century and we have to do with what we have, so it's really important not to say we want to get away. The children are incarnating into this place because in a certain way they originated it. The children come to the place that had been originated in their own thought life, way back. They want to work on this time, that's why they come now. So the question is "How can we make them strong enough to work with the time that is materialistic, without getting shattered by the materialism itself before they are able to do that?"

When Rudolf Steiner talked to young people in 1923, fairly late in his life, he talked about this materialism as a dragon. He put it in a picture, saying that the breath of the dragon is all over the globe now. You cannot get out of it. You cannot get to an island or on a mountain, because even there you will feel that the air has become thin. So it is not about moving out of it but moving forward. How can we move forward into our future? How do we protect that which needs to be protected, without making the children afraid of our time? By not being afraid yourself, because the way you stand in the world will be an imprint on their way of thinking too; you are their door to the world. So if you are afraid of the world, and try to move out of it, that will be part of their makeup. That's not what we want. We are here to work in the world and on the world.

> *A question about sorting out what to keep and let go—when do we stop doing that and start looking over the whole of life?*

I think it is finished when we are fourteen, that by that age we are moving more actively toward what we have to meet. But it comes in stages.

> *Comment: A help toward fearlessness is talking to others outside the Waldorf world who hunger to validate their feelings. There is a need to find words to speak to others in a true way.*

Steiner was suffering from the same thing: that he felt that people got stuck on the same words. He said if he could he would change the name "Anthroposophy" every week. So it's not Steiner, it's us.

> *What is the relationship between wrestling with passages in Steiner, and Jung's sitting in the sand?*

Nice question. To struggle with a passage, you have to slow down, to sit with it. It's the same inner strength you need. Observation and thinking both belong to our head pole, to the nerve/sense pole. When we observe, we sense, we do not think; and when we think we do not sense. We have to be able to live in both, and then they will enhance each other because the nerve/sense functions belong together; they are only separated in us. To be able to observe without thinking, and then to think so hard that we are not being pulled out by the sensing, that is very important. It's the same.

> *A request for advice on how to help young mothers whose babies aren't sleeping, even if they seem to be in a rich, media-free, healthy environment.*

When you read Rudolf Steiner's biography, you find that he was actually colicy; when he was little he was screaming a lot. You have to have compassion for a big soul being in a small body!

There are many things to talk about sleep, and I wouldn't do it justice to just brush it off, because before you can give advice you need to give a proper diagnosis. You need to know why he doesn't sleep, and not say, "You are doing something wrong." It could be that he hasn't overcome his birth trauma yet…it might be that the organs have not adapted to the food yet. I do not know. It might be something in the mother's milk that he cannot digest, or no mother's milk. You can tell the mother that it would be important to know why he doesn't sleep, instead of feeling that she is doing something wrong. She herself might be beginning to be afraid when she puts him down, or there might be too much closeness.

This is something I haven't touched on yet, how much alone time the children need. When Steiner talks about thinking, which for a very young child is observing, he says that they need to be hermits, for these first stages of thinking. They need to be hermits; they need to be alone. Today I see children not having enough alone time any more. This doesn't mean that you shut them into a room and lock the door; it means that you are able to move away and do your work. I know there are many questions about that, but this alone time, that doesn't mean leaving them alone; you are close by, but also your thoughts are not all the time sitting on them in fear.

You know as kindergarten teachers that the way you can survive your day is not by thinking all the time about where the children are. You carry them in your etheric, you actually feel them in your etheric, and then you know where they are. If you would have to look for them all the time you would go crazy, and the children too. So parents can learn that. The first child is the hardest because you are so conscious of everything. After five, you know how to do it.

> *Question: How early does that start, that alone time?*

I don't say any more "This is when it needs to be." There is this relationship between mother and child, where the mother needs to be helped to trust that she is still there even if she moves away. Attachment parenting doesn't mean that the children have to be attached all the time. Because they *are* attached. It's more that you trust that attachment; but for a first-time mother that needs time. It's about how I can help the mother to trust that she actually is attached.

If I have a consultation with parents today most of the time fathers come too, which is wonderful. I simply explain that children need to practice using their movement body by being on the floor and trying it out. You cannot do everything in a sling. So that's when it starts. How much time that needs depends on the child too. Some children want to be left alone, and others are a little bit more clingy. What's the reason? There are memories from a previous lifetime, too, that they still carry. As a mother your goal is not to push them away, it's more to set the child forth in freedom.

I tell the parents to talk to each other at night: How did the day go? What can we do differently tomorrow? This has such a strong effect on the children, when they feel mother and father actually both carrying them.

And then—the child actually shows you. I'm not so "German" any more. My students help me.

> *Within Waldorf programs too, there is the need to find that alone time.*

That's right. Play, alone time; they need to have secrets. Even the very little ones, they need to have a place where they are not observed all the time. We are so afraid that they will do bad things that we don't allow that any more.

So, did we get to thinking? In the second year of life, along with naming, the young child develops a sense-feeling of the concept, a sense that the name and the object belong together. As adults, we look at the object and we name it and we take it for granted that they belong together. But the children first have to put them together. And then they put one concept and another concept in a new relationship, and that is thinking. They actually have to stand on their feet in order to do that, because you have to have a *standpoint* for thinking.

If you've ever seen a young child meeting her own hands, looking from one to the other, this is what will bring thinking about: to be able to put two concepts into a relationship. That's the beginning of thinking. But then it's released, it's free of the doing it: they can just think it. First they have to do it, then they have to name it, and then they think it.

In the beginning, they put two concepts together that we would never put together. They have the innovative, creative, relational thinking which is the pre-requisite for being a good scientist. Good physicists are relational thinkers. They are not intellectual. That's why Waldorf students are so well-liked in colleges and universities, because they not just taught concepts but are given the time to learn: first the picture, and out of that comes the alphabet. That needs time, and that keeps the ability to think creatively. It's not just letting the children wait until they are ready.

In kindergarten you already start to help the children think. Before you have them in kindergarten they already start to think, not only in grade school. So the time you give them between recognizing something and naming it and then putting the two together, that is thinking. And if you do not put your own concepts on them—"No, that's not how it is; *that's* how it is"—they might discover something completely new.

And in order to do it, you have to be willing to let go of your judgments too. As adults, we practice thinking by being in a faculty meeting, and when it's the hardest you learn the most. There's this guy who always says the same thing and you cannot hear it any more and you'd rather leave the school than listen to this guy one more time. Do this exercise which is so hard: remove your feelings, and see what is he is trying to say and think it. I have such a hard time with that because I am so emotional. But through that you learn thinking.

And if you want to do it more consequentially, then do the concentration exercise in these six so-called subsidiary exercises that Steiner gave. They are so beautifully put together in *Stairway of Surprise* by Michael Lipson. People think "Oh, that's so boring," but it's not boring. One of the exercises is to practice a soft gaze, that you look at an object and try to look at it really, every crook and cranny, everything that is in there, and give it a name. And then you look totally softly on it. And you change from the more exact to the soft, back and forth. That will practice your versatility and letting go of judgment.

And go to the artists in your community—do clay modeling, or painting, or singing. For me clay modeling is most important because I can feel what I do. Going through a process, an artistic process, will also help you to think.

So there are lots of opportunities to make good what we have not been able to do ourselves, and that we can do with large groups of people. Then we do not have to talk about the ether body or the astral body, we just do it. In art all the things that a young child does come together again, for us.

Anything else about thinking? Did you get the feeling for thinking?

> *A comment on the practice of sitting in silence and watching thoughts, to step out of oneself.*

That's the point of the concentration exercise, to be able to put your will in concentrating and then observe how your thoughts pass by all the time.

> *What is the difference between percept and concept?*

It's hardly possible for us as adults to experience it any more, because we perceive and we immediately give it a concept. So it's very hard. You get an inkling of it when you feel something or taste something you do not know. You try to find the concept. Then you have a true perception for a moment. But we cannot live without conceptualizing; that's who we are as adults. When you observe so-called handicapped people, who cannot do that so fast, you can actually see how their perception is still much more pure than in us, with our brains.

> *A participant struggles with parents who come in and explain everything to the child.*

Have parent evenings, without judging. Parents want to do the best for their child, they do not want to harm the child. There can be big conferences just for parents, the same content we have here, but for parents.

The parents she would want to come don't come to the evenings.

Then you do have to do it. Very carefully, not by preaching but through observation. You simply explain what you see. It's a very slow and humble process, working with parents. If not, then they do not want to listen to you any more.

My parent work started to be different when I stopped judging. So as long as we are in what they do and what we do better, they cannot hear it. You have to be really open to what the parents think. I find a lot of judgment in myself too.

A question about how thinking and willing can support each other.

For young children, the thinking and the willing are still very close. What they think, they also feel, and act on it. The younger they are, the more immediate the connection. Then when we explain the thinking, when we put our dry thinking into the children's thinking, they start to not act on their thinking any more. And then you have children who stand there, who observe the players but are just not able to play. The thinking has separated from that artistic process of acting on the thought itself.

So, play, play, play, play, play!

By the way, when I say "play," children rolling in mud is also play. And children getting wet and dirty, as uncomfortable as may be because you have to clean up again—for some children who are in their heads, that is perception again. That is total perception, with the whole body.

The repetition of your stories, which you often repeat for two weeks, takes courage because the children complain: "The same story again…" But it's not that the children need a new story, it's that you have to enliven the story first. If you cannot see the pictures any more, the children cannot feel the story any more. Thinking is also creating, and the young child is still creating pictures, creating imaginations. It's not thoughts like we have. They still see what they think. And that's still the case for a long time. Thinking for the young child is still imaginative thinking.

The last part of this talk I would like to dedicate to the senses. Part of learning to walk, learning to speak, learning to think, is that we have senses. Without the senses we wouldn't have any of these human abilities. So without having the time to go into details, I want to remind you of the preciousness of the senses. And I want to link that with what I did yesterday afternoon about the relationship between early and later life, because as we get older the senses fade again. So as they are just coming in and develop, as we get older they fade again. We see less and hearing is a little bit harder and our balance gets off. How humbling it is to let go of what you thought was your right to have. By coming into it and living it fully it might be easier to humbly and gracefully let go of it again.

The world the child can sense is the world in which he lives. It sounds so trite. The world we sense is the world in which we live, and if we do not sense it, it's not there. There's a whole world we do not sense that is there: the supersensible world. It's there, but we cannot sense it, we don't have the sense organs yet for it. But we have here the physical world, we have physical senses. And as much as we can, we need to protect and develop and foster these senses, so that the world of the child is as rich as possible. If there are senses missing, there is a part of the world missing. Not figuratively, literally: part of the world is missing.

And one of the largest senses, so to speak, is the sense of touch, because our whole body is the sense organ: the skin and under the skin. It's very finely tuned. Our sense of touch is the sense that has already in it as a seed the ability to sense that the other person is an I. The sense of ego is like a seed in the sense of touch.

And what do we discover through the sense of touch? That it's two-sided: on the one hand, through the sense of touch we discover that we are, because when you sitting there feel your bottom and your back and your feet, you actually feel "I am there." And the more you move out of a whole-body experience of "I am there," the more you are sitting in a tower, the less you are participating in the world. So the more you are able to feel with your whole body, the more you are able to feel as a whole person, as a whole being in the world. If you feel yourself as a whole being in the world, then you feel trust in the world. And when you feel trust in the world, when you feel the ground under your feet, you feel the Father-ground, and that is a feeling of God. It's such an existential feeling of God, that for the child it is immediate: it's not conscious, yet. It's not "God" sitting up there, it's a full-body experience of God.

And if that is interrupted, if that is not fostered or protected, then on our journey we lose it again. We lose that existential feeling of God. We have to go through the dark night of the soul, to go through being without God in order to find ourselves. That's our journey. It's like Parzival, who has to leave the mother. He starts to leave the mother when he kills the bird, and he realizes that he has killed for the first time. That is letting go, but first we have to have it.

So the sense of touch is very important to be nurtured for the young child, by having the child close. You are the doorway through which the world is experienced. But then, it's important to let the child go in the right moment, so that he discovers her own sense of touch, his own skin, and not only senses through your skin.

I have intense, passionate conversations, mostly with my students, about nursing. Rudolf Steiner says mother's milk is the only substance that can wake up the head forces, the consciousness forces, the thinking forces, in the child by means of—now it is not the sense of touch, it is the sense of taste. And he says the sense of taste in the young child is something we cannot understand any more when we are older. The child tastes with the full body, from inside now. This tasting is not only the substance of mother's milk, it's also the whole essence of "mother" that is in the mother's milk: mother's intentions, mother's astrality, mother's feelings, actually go with mother's milk. And that has to stop at a certain point too. Not because Steiner said so. Steiner never talked about that, actually, that you have to stop at a certain point. He just said that this is what happens, and then you have to find when it is time to set the child free even on that level. And that is for every child a little bit different. Sometimes the mother needs it a little longer, when the child is already ready.

Again, this is not a place of knowing better or preaching, it's a place of sharing information. I share what I know and ask what you think about what I know. And then mothers and fathers can make their own decisions. You see the difference? So this outer touch and this inner tasting have to separate; if not, we as adults are always pulled by our senses. We are not free from our sense impressions. We have to be able to separate from tasting and smelling and touching.

Handicapped children who always have to touch everything and lick everything, even when they are older—that is the place of the very young child, not the older child. Our sensory body is there to inform us about the world, but then at a certain point we have to be able to separate from it. And the fuller the child has an experience of the sense world, the easier it is then to let go of it, because the senses complement each other. It's like a temple of senses. If there is one part of the temple missing, we hold onto the other parts. But if we give the child the impression of the wholeness of sensory integration, then it's easier to step in and out of the temple.

The bodily senses are the senses of touch, movement, balance, and life, the vital sense. The sense of vitality is strengthened through not having it all the time. Having it—and not having it. The vital sense needs to feel that there is an end, that there is a fullness and an emptiness. So the children who are deprived of everything show deficiency in vitality, and the children who have everything also show signs of deficiency in the vital sense. They get cranky, unhappy, depressed, and you ask why? That might be the reason behind some sleep problems too, that there is a time for having and there is a time for not having, and that actually helps the vital sense.

You can look at yourself, also for yourself, how to strengthen your own vital sense. We always complain that we are run down and tired and don't have enough, but when I look at my own life I see that I don't have enough times where I *don't* do, I *don't* have. I run all the time without stopping. This is a different kind of rhythmical life for the adult and for the child. So to strengthen the vital sense you need a rhythm of having/not having, of day and night, of cold and warmth, of meals. Nice things, and sometimes painful things. You, as adults, can find your own rhythm in your day too.

The sense of movement I already touched on when I talked about how important it is for the child to practice with the movement body, which at the same time practices the inner sense of balance, having to find the sense of balance.

These are the bodily senses. They are the foundation for proper functioning of the so-called world senses or the senses that are connected to the other human being. There is the sense not only of hearing sounds, but of being able to make the word out of sounds. We have children who do not understand any more what adults say. They do not get it. Their hearing is fine, but they do not put the sounds together as words. They do not have the sense for the word.

And then they might understand the word, but the thought content of the word also has to be picked up properly: the sense of thought. And then the last, the one that has to do with the sense of touch: the sense of the ego of the other human being. In the moment we meet each other, we realize, bodily, that there is another human being.

So these senses are, for the young child, in your care. And you have to ask yourself almost every day: Did I work with all the senses? The middle senses are the senses of sight, smell, taste and warmth. Did I work with these senses today in a conscious way?

And then you have already so much to work with as early childhood educators. You do not need specialists in your classroom. How do I work with the senses? Are they integrated in the children? Why does my one boy always have to touch another child? Doesn't he have a feeling of touch inside? Why do some children have to spin around? Maybe there is something with the inner sense of balance? Why are some cranky all the time? If you don't feel at home in your body how can you be happy? It's very unsettling not to be at home in your body.

And that again is what we learn by feeling how it is to grow older, when you get cranky old people, because the body is not a home any more, and we have to work with that consciously. The old person and the child recognize each other, immediately. The children look at me, and they know I know, and I look at them and I know they know. So there is a new relationship that forms, which is quite touching.

> *A participant described a child who is scooting as opposed to crawling. She tried taking cushions of the sofa for the child to crawl over—but she will avoid them and only stay on the flat surface. She is crying a lot.*

It would be really good to look at the phases of child development in movement, to see what comes first, and then to do it with her. She can go down on the floor with the parents every night for half an hour, doing joyfully the movements that she has missed. The father and mother might not be able to do them either.

> *What is the relationship between children who are very allergic and have skin complaints, and the sense of touch?*

It's not that a missing sense of touch will result in allergies of the skin, no. That's not the relationship. But afflictions of the skin have an impact on the sense of touch, yes. The skin is the safest organ for the body to work things out. As long as things are worked out on the skin, I'm actually quite happy. When they turn inside, then it's more dangerous. With the skin, you have to see what in the body is too hot.

> *Is that generally the cause of skin conditions?*

Yes. If it itches, then we are with something too hot. There are other skin conditions that are too cold. But that which itches and is red, it's too hot.

> *Even if the skin is cool to the touch?*

Yes, that doesn't matter.

There are many thin-skinned children today. Here you can work with the sense of touch, with the sense of warmth, with playfulness, with daring things, so that they dare to do something, not holding back in anxiety. You cannot push them, but they need to feel safe in their skin, so holding them, wrapping them, will be important. And giving them the feeling of safety, which they need in order to go out.

It is interesting that they are often the ones that are underdressed.

Yes. Actually the thin-skinned children are often sweating a little bit. You first have to help them to feel that the skin is safe place, and then they can be dressed again.

Birth of the Imagination
PART I

I am very excited to talk about the birth of the imagination, and I want to thank the people who brought me here, because the preparation for it was really worth the whole event. I hope that I am able to ignite that kind of enthusiasm for the imagination in you too.

In order for you to understand the birth of the imagination, we need to do a lot of preparatory work on what imagination is. There's a lot of confusion between imagination and picture and mental picture. The title "Birth of the Imagination" is not completely correct, because we are born out of the imagination from the very first moment we come out of the world of pictures. We are born into a world without pictures. And then when we die we go back into a picture-world. But here in this earth, we are actually in a picture-less world, and we have to make the pictures.

In the spiritual world, where we come from, pictures are beings that are in constant transformation, constant movement. And the memory of these pictures is what the child is born with. But it's a memory that's not conscious; it's a bodily memory, a deep-in-the-soul memory that needs to be awakened, and not only awakened, but transformed.

So we come out of a world of pictures, and we go into a world of pictures, and here we are in a picture-less world.

Before I go to the young child, I actually would like to go to the old person. We have called this series of conferences "Cradle of a Healthy Life." And I would like to lead you to old age. It is actually getting earlier and earlier, that people have no ability any more to digest or transform the pictures. That leads to dementia.

Dementia is actually an etheric body, a life body, that is so full of untransformed pictures and experiences that it gets stiff. Since the life body is also the place where we imprint our memories, no memories can be imprinted.

It's like your email is full. Nothing can be imprinted any more, so the person with dementia goes back further and further trying to bring out pictures and experiences from earlier life, but instead of being able to transform and digest these, they become the content of the experience. The older person with beginning dementia starts to live in these old experiences more and more. And they themselves become stiff pictures.

So you see that to work with what to do in early childhood with pictures and imagination is of paramount importance for later life. Going back to the young child, I want to pick up a little bit what we did when we talked about the first three years of life. Children are born in complete sympathy for the world that they are born into, full of imaginations from the place they come from. And through sympathy, flowing into the world, they start to move the world inside. So imitation in the first year is like merging with the outside world and in a way comparing it with the pictures in the inside world. And then, since they do not match completely, they try to adjust—and this is not conscious, this is completely in the will. This is a complete sympathetic-empathetic merging with the world, and trying to make sense of it, or adjusting to a world that does not make complete sense.

For the young child, for the infant in the first year, then the world itself reveals itself as Imagination—but Imagination of the will. Imagination of the creative kind. That which is in the world outside is actually forming the child him- or herself. We are now in the area of imaginations that are creative, formative powers.

The child comes out of a world of pictures that come from before birth, and now meets a world that reveals itself to the child as imaginations, but they are imaginations that are alive and creative. And that forms the child.

And then when uprightness has been achieved, can you imagine what kind of impression an upright human being is for a child who lives in intense will activity? What kind of joy it will be when it matches this picture of uprightness, of an upright human being, with inner experience? That is the joy of the ten-month-old, eleven-month-old, twelve-month-old who finally can stand up and walk. There is something that matches inside.

And then in the second year of life, at first it's not speech yet—it's sounds that are forming out of a playful practicing with the lips and the arms and the whole body. The speech that lives in gestures starts to be internalized and stilled, and words can be formed. So that the gesture—now you have to think eurythmically—the gesture of something that is round and whole becomes a "*B*" or a "ball." For a young child the experience of language is intensely imaginative, intensely experienced. We cannot even think any more how intense the experience of—again—the matching of the gesture and the word is for the young child.

And then, when that has happened, naming can start. And with the naming the capacity of language, of expressive language. It starts with the experience of "bbbbb" and "mmmmmm" when they are still lying in the crib, making bubbles. We cannot entirely fathom what a deep soul-body experience this is, how enjoyable it is.

These are all the foundations of imagination. The birth of imagination does not happen in the middle years alone. That's when imagination is used to play and to experience the world, but we will look at that a little bit later.

When language and naming have happened, and language has gotten so far that this whole body-soul experience of a word can be externalized, and the child actually can look at the object that this word encompasses from outside, then a mental image is possible. A mental image—do you know what it is? It's not alive any more. It's objectified. It leads to the concept. So we have a gesture of antipathy, that comes with the possibility to build mental images and then to come to the concept.

Then in the second and third year, out of two concepts the child makes a new connection that is not repeated from what has been heard from the parents. The child puts one concept and another together in a completely new connection, and that is thought. They are incredibly interesting thoughts that a children have at that age, when they put concepts together in a way you would not even dream of, which is incredibly alive.

So that is briefly what happens in these three years in regard to walking, speaking, and thinking. You see how the pictures with which the child comes start to "cool." They first cool into the word, and then into the concept, the mental picture. It's a cooling movement, an antipathy movement.

If the child is not allowed to work on these inner pictures that are matched with the outside world but experienced inside, if they are not allowed to bring these pictures up and let them out, then these pictures that are not put into the use of either language and thought, or later used in play, and matched with the outside world, then it is an experience of unrest. Not being able to concentrate, not being able to imitate, not being able to be fully a child, not being able to be completely in sympathy. It's like an undigested piece of meat in the stomach, and when we have an undigested piece of meat in our stomach, then we are not able to fully be a human being. But we come back to this later again.

Now we have to look to the other side. In the second lecture of *Study of Man* Steiner speaks about how imagination is born, the nature of imagination. In order to understand the nature of imagination we have to go to the other side. That side is then not connected to our thinking—antipathy, mental pictures, concepts—but connected to our will, our sympathy.

To understand the will is not so easy, as you know, because it's that in us which is most unconscious. But you realize that when you carry something, in order to hold it, your will has to engage over and over and over. I'm holding this glass, I'm in my arm, and my will engages over and over again. It's a constant activation of my will.

So this will works in us, or is necessary in us, in order to think. When we have will in thinking, we can concentrate. We are able to put one thought in a logical connection to the other. That is one form of will in thinking. If there is no will in thinking, we find children who cannot concentrate and cannot stay with anything.

The will in the movement system is basically there in order that we are moved. If there is no will, the children cannot move. And what is the will in the feeling? The will in the feeling is there so that we are able to be interested, to have enthusiasm and interest in the world. So you see that whereas on the antipathy side we project everything inside, we realize it, we feel it on the inside, now the gesture is going to the outside. It's being interested, being in the world. Here it's in my inner world, where we can become toxic from our own pictures; and here it is that we are actually starting to move outside, into the world.

And this movement, this gesture, this capacity of sympathy to move outside—if that gets intensified it actually turns back on itself and starts to create in itself, and that is imagination, or in German "phantasie."

I will say it again. When you get the feeling for the nature of the will—the will in us that is our innermost, most individual, human capacity—you see that this will is not there to save ourselves; the will is there to connect to another. Remember that the child comes into the world with incredible will. This incredible will is the power of imitation. It's the interest in the world in the way that everything that is around is imitated, even the tiniest gesture, the finest vibration of tone. The child builds up him- or herself, and takes what he or she needs and brings it into the body. Can you start to get a feeling for the quality of will?

Then, in the threefold human being, if this will, in the service of thinking and feeling and movement, gets intensified but then creates within itself, that is the power of imagination.

Does anyone have a better picture than I? Can you see it? Can you help me? What does that look like?

> *A comment: A child watching mom or dad cooking, taking it in as an image, then reenacting it in play.*

The power of imagination is what the children have in such abundance when they are allowed to play.

> *Another comment: A picture of leaven or yeast, something bringing about expansion and movement.*

There's a lot of will in the yeast. Any other pictures?

> *A participant spoke of the difference between saying "You may put the car away" and "Can you park the car in the garage?" when putting the toys away. The "garage" is just a table...but for the child it awakens interest. Language is connected to will; the right words can awaken that interest in the children so that they want to do something.*

Can you see that this power of the imagination, this power of the will, that can go in a positive way, or into a negative, destructive way, and how important it is for children today that we provide them with the right pictures, the right activities. Activities can be pictures too. Tomorrow we will talk about what it means to speak in pictures, or live in pictures. But if you provide something so that this will has a way to work in a constructive way, you see what kind of power that means.

In the last twenty years I have seen completely new illnesses in my offices. There are children with compulsive disorders, children who are destructive in the classroom; they cannot control their temper any more. I was hearing on the radio how many children are put on medication because they cannot control their impulses. And you realize that the true nature of bipolar disorders is that the will is not helped into the right direction. We will speak about that tomorrow.

So again, it is important that we understand that the child who wants to live in the world brings impulses—the children of today have moral impulses, they want to work in the world—that live in the soul as pictures. If these pictures are not brought up into the feeling life of the child, the astral body, if they stay in the ether body and not brought up into the astral body through play, through stories, then what happens? In Lecture 16 of *Spiritual Science as a Foundation for Social Forms*, Steiner says:

> *The souls who descend through conception and birth into earthly life bring along for themselves images from the spiritual world. When pictures are brought along out of spiritual existence into physical life, and if salvation is to arise for the human being and his social life, they must under all circumstances be united with the astral body, whereas the element lacking images only unites with the ego.*
>
> *It is predominantly the unfolding of the ego which has blossomed in humanity since the fifteenth century. Now, however, the time is beginning when man has to feel: Within me there live pictures from my prenatal existence; during my earthly life, I have to make them come alive. I cannot accomplish this merely with my ego; I must work deeper into myself, and this must reach as far as my astral body."*

Now what do these words mean? How can we get these pictures up out of our life body, up into our astral body, our feeling body? Here we have the profound necessity for play in kindergarten. It is important that the child brings up the pictures from inside, plays them out, and by playing, experiences what has been lying in the soul as pictures.

> **A story from a mother who arranged a playdate: she wanted to plan what activities to do, but her little girl just said, "I'm going to be the princess, he's going to be the knight, and we are going to kiss."**

Tomorrow we are going to talk more about play, and I hope you will bring more of these wonderful examples, because that is your domain. You are privileged to see the children playing out their inner pictures, and that is something that is sacred. You are actually in the face of the spiritual world when you watch children play. This feeling of happiness when you watch them — that is something you know better than I, I only see very little of that. I don't have grandchildren yet.

Back to imagination: the birth of imagination actually leads us also into the history of humanity. Imagination is not so old. Imagination is what replaced the old clairvoyance, when people were still connected to the spiritual world and experienced the pictures immediately. This kind of immediate living in the world of pictures changed about 300 years before Christ. Around that time, the human being was no longer able to look into the spiritual world in the same way as before, to get the spiritual pictures immediately. When you look at the art before that time, you see that there is something that connects.

So with the birth of the imagination, around 300 years before Christ, we find that the human being has to recreate the pictures that lie at the depth of the soul. You see through art how that happens. The study of the evolution of consciousness through art is a wonderful way to see how imagination was used, to remember where we came from.

Then comes the time around the Middle Ages when this creative imagination starts to wane. These creative pictures are not present in the same way any more. And then came the Renaissance—Renaissance means rebirth. And so it was a re-picturing. It was a repetition of what had been done before. Artists repeated, rebirthed what was there before, and made it more personal.

For the Greek person, in Western culture, the temple, the architecture itself, embodied the god. Now look today how far we have come from the time when our buildings embodied the spirit, the god. Are they still able to? Can you see that this ability to create—out of the inner pictures, out of the imagination—forms, buildings, pictures, sculptures, that embody the spirit, not as a mental image, but as creative pictures—has waned, and we no longer even remember it properly any more.

Why? In a picture-less time we can only recreate what was there before, and connect it more and more with the sense impressions that we have in the world. And then you see the culminations of sense impressions in the Baroque and Rococo. It's very hard to be in an over-richly decorated place and still have the feeling that this is the embodiment of a spiritual being.

When Rudolf Steiner conceived and built the first Goetheanum, that was what he wanted to bring: a building that in itself, through its form, gave a living place for the spirit. So when you entered the building and when you went through the building you felt the living spirit.

When you look at the human being, you actually see a living form for the spirit, for the human spirit. From the very first moment—that would be another topic, to look at embryology—the human form, in itself, is not only an expression, but a habitation for the spirit.

All of this is what the child is experiencing unconsciously, and then having to forget. The living pictures have to re-awaken what lies inside. That is schooling. That is what the educator has to do.

As early childhood educators, you have to ask how much time do the children stay outside? How much time do the children need to actually play what they have experienced outside? If even these wonderful pictures that are found outside, in nature, are not transformed in play, they are pictures that lie inside the child. Think about that.

Early childhood educators are the people who need to know the most about the physiology, the anatomy, the psychology of the child. Early childhood teachers do not only need to have a healthy soul any more. You need to understand what you see, so that in your choices for the children in the kindergarten you lay a foundation for a healthy soul, a healthy body, and a free spirit.

> *What happens when the impressions are not transformed in the child?*

They turn into restlessness, impulsiveness. An etheric body that is more and more stiff. Allergies. Digestive disorders. Anxieties. Lack of interest, being too "full." So you see that if you understand the nature of imagination, the nature of the pictures, you touch the root of many other complaints of children today. And you will be able to address them in a different way, not with another specialist, but in the way you actually conduct your kindergarten.

> *Are there two different kinds of pictures that come into the etheric body: the pictures that are brought across the threshold at birth, and then pictures that come from the other side?*

Yes. These imprints come from two sides. New experiences are also imprinted.

> *And the pictures they bring with them—are these forming the body and the physical organs?*

They should inform the will. Remember that Steiner said they are moral pictures. They determine what the soul came to do in the world.

> *Are these images that are living in the soul worked out at all during sleep?*

Yes. But you know, children today have many sleep disorders. Nightmares, sleep anxieties, fears.

> *When the images the children bring with them meet other images*

> that come from media, are they images that are stored as well and can't be digested? Do you think that is why there is more dementia?

I do think so, yes. When the etheric body becomes stiff, then the physical structures are not enlivened any more, not refreshed any more. Then you find that there are brain formations that become like tendons; they become matter forms, too much matter. Bones, almost.

> I have children who stutter; they want to say a word but can't. Is that related to the feeling?

Sometimes with children who stutter you find that there is so much will, so much impulse to express, that the instrument cannot follow that intense will. Children who stutter have an intense will. You have to divert the will in movement, out of that intention to speak. Then they can speak.

> I am struck by the children who are holding back stool, as early as six weeks of age. Could that also be a symptom of weakened etheric forces?

Holding back stool is a picture that they have formed, an imagination that is not helpful. That is that "The world is not safe, so I don't give anything from the inside to the outside, I hold it back." Most of the time there is something that is way too much for the feeling body, for the child to be able to process. It's not a weak etheric body, it's an imagination that has become physical: "The world is not safe."

> Could you comment on the arts and the etheric body of the teacher?

What does the teacher need to do to be of service to the child with regard to images? What kind of picture life or artistic life? Not that you have to be a painter or a sculptor; a teacher has to be an artist in the way he or she teaches. What kind of qualities does a teacher need?

The teacher as an artist is the closest an adult can come to the playing child. In art, as in play, an inner picture is brought outside and put in relationship to an outer reality. So if the teacher needs to be able to bring an inner picture to expression that has a relationship to the reality of the outside world. In the lower grades it's the stories themselves; the teacher doesn't have to do much. A fairy tale is a picture; it's complete. But then the way you teach the letters can be deadening, or it can be enlivening. So when you bring a sound to the experience of the child and then relate it to something in the outside world, that is real. Like the "*B*" and the ball.

Or the "*Ffffff*" that has a flowing character when we speak it, with the fish, then this picture guides the child to the letter. It's an inner experience that relates, in truth, to the outer picture.

How we do that in early childhood? That will be our topic tomorrow. How do we help the child to bring these inner pictures into a truthful relation to the outer reality? Think about that in the night.

Other questions?

> *What about children who are losing their teeth earlier?*

It's more individual than ever; the coming and the losing of teeth is much more irregular than ever. That shows me where the child lives. Are they finished with their form and show now "I'm done?" It's not the losing of the teeth, it's when they push out their first tooth that has not been there before: the six-year molar. If that comes earlier, then it shows that this child is really in a hurry to get done. When they have built their form, transformed the inherited body, then as a sign there is this tooth that was not there before: "I'm done, now something else can come." Then the forces are freed for learning. And these children, they are able to learn. We cannot hold them back.

> *What are the differences in sleep between a child that has transformed experiences through play and one who hasn't?*

In the night, like all of us, the child meets the angel. The day is reviewed, and for the children they have a choice of what they take in and what they do not. If they took in everything it would be completely overwhelming. So that is always a consolation with children in horrible circumstances: they do not take in everything. They can say, "This is what I need according to my destiny." It is like when you eat a heavy meal in the evening; the children are staying too close to their bodies. When they have nightmares and wake up many times in the night, that shows that they are too close, they cannot leave completely. So the difference is, that if you have digested your pictures properly, you can go really fast and look over your day. If you haven't, you are still body-bound.

> *Does that have to do with the faster pace of modern life, the overscheduling, that there is not enough time at night?*

You can see for yourself: when I do too much in the day I cannot sleep at night. I am so restless that I have the feeling that I do not really refresh.

> *At what age does the child take the experiences of the day into sleep?*

This is what we need to teach them. In the beginning what the child needs to learn is to sleep, and to breathe. So this totally depends on how we support the sleeping process.

Do you have enough to take into your own sleep? There are two pictures I would like to leave with you of the imagination. One, Christof Wiechert mentioned at the World Teachers Conference in 2004, which was all about imagination. So what I've learned there, I bring here.

He mentioned how imagination in Greek mythology, the birth of the imagination was actually told. Medusa was a Gorgon, a hideous being, and this being of the Gorgon, Medusa, stood for this old clairvoyant connection to the spiritual world, that was in itself creative. In the spiritual world, nothing is dead. Everything is created every moment. So when we are in the spiritual world we are not free to stop and reflect; we are part of the creation all the time. In order to come to thinking, to a self-consciousness, this Medusa had to be killed. And it was Perseus who took the task to behead Medusa. But he knew that when he would look at Medusa, the power of the creation was so strong that he would lose consciousness and would turn to stone. So the only way he could behead Medusa was to look into his shield, which was shining, and see the head of the Gordon and by looking into it behead her.

Can you see the image for how we form mental pictures and concepts? It shows how we have mirror pictures, not real pictures, in order to do that. So out of the severed neck of Medusa, Pegasus opened his wings and flew. But what is often not mentioned is that behind Pegasus (representing poetry) came another being, and that was Imagination. Imagination was given to us as a healing, a kind of bridge between what had to die, to be beheaded, and that which was made possible: to look into the mirror. So that is one picture to take into the night.

The other is found in one of Rudolf Steiner's Mystery Dramas, in scene six of the third drama, *The Guardian of the Threshold.*

There is an older lady who has the power to tell wonderful stories, stories that are alive with truth. She tells this story about Imagination, while the forces of Lucifer and Ahriman are present, or have been present. She tells the story of imagination — in German it is *Phantasie*:

> *Once on a time there lived a child of God*
> *Who had affinity with those who weave*
> *The thoughtful wisdom of the spirit-realms.*
> *This child, brought up by truth's almighty Sire*

Grew up within his realm to ancient strength.
And when his body, radiant with light,
Did feel his ripened will creative stir,
He often looked with pity on the Earth
Where souls of men were striving after truth.
Then to the Sire of truth the child would say:
'The souls of men are thirsting for the drink
Which thou canst hand to them from out thy springs.'
With earnest speech the Sire of truth replied:
'The springs, of which I am appointed guard,
Let light stream forth from out the spirit-suns;
Only such beings dare to drink the light
As need not thirst for air that they may breathe.
Therefore in light have I brought up a child
Who can feel pity for the souls on Earth
And manifest the light 'midst breathing men.
So turn and go unto mankind and bring
The light that's in their souls to meet my light
Enfilled with confidence and spirit-life.'
So then the shining light-child turned, and went
To souls who keep themselves alive by breath.
And many good men found he on the Earth,
Who offered him with joy their souls' abode.
These souls he turned to gaze with grateful love
Upon their Sire who dwells in springs of light.
And when the child heard from the lips of men
And joyous mind of men, the magic word
Of fantasy, he knew himself alive
Dwelling with gladness in the hearts of men.
But one sad day there came unto the child
A man who cast upon him chilling looks.
'I turn the souls of men on earth toward
The Sire of truth who dwells in springs of light —'
Thus to the strange man did the light-child speak.
The man replied: 'Thou dost but weave wild dreams
Into men's spirits, and deceiv'st their souls.'
And since the day which witnessed this event
The child who can bring light to breathing souls
Hath often suffered slander from mankind.

Birth of the Imagination
PART II

There is not a lack of love for the young child in the world. There is a lot of love—not just in our circles. There is not a lack of good and loving teachers for young children in the world. What are missing are the imaginations of the true nature of the child.

We are fortunate that Rudolf Steiner gave us the imaginations to understand the child in his or her true nature. In this being fortunate, we have the responsibility to use these imaginations to come alive in us, and not just for our little lovely home kindergarten and school, but so that they radiate out into the world. Because that is what true imaginations do. So the *Study of Man* is not only for grade school teachers. It is paramount for early childhood teachers, because there you find your imaginations for what you do in kindergarten.

We are seeds for the future, cultural seeds, as Waldorf early childhood teachers, as anthroposophists. Then we fructify the future, and then we are true helpers of Rudolf Steiner. And there is nothing old about it. It's incredibly new. We do not even really understood the amount or the richness of imaginations, seed-imaginations for the future, that lie in *Study of Man* and others of Steiner's works. This notion that they are dry is actually only our laziness to digest it, to take the seed that lies in the imagination and make it alive. There is nothing dry about anthroposophy or Rudolf Steiner.

As early childhood teachers, the children bring you the fresh forces, the fresh hope, the pictures, and want you to make whole what they had to sever when they were born into a form. One of the pictures that lies deep in the soul of the child and that has to be reawakened, is that everything is connected. We are all connected, and we have to find out in what way, not just use buzzwords like "We are all one." It becomes a deed: how can we reconnect what is severed, what is disconnected?

And that part in us that reconnects the things, that makes them whole again, is also the humble servant and organ of imagination. That is the heart. Rudolf Steiner describes it in a picture: if we would put the tiniest dwarf right in the center of the heart, what this tiny being would see would be the same as when we imagine the whole of the universe. In the heart, the whole universe is held as a picture, as a reality.

So today, I hope that we can come a little bit closer to a true understanding of this power of imagination and the responsibility we have to guard it through what we do in the early childhood years, and later in the grade school, *and* in the high school, *and* in life. We can only understand anything, truly understand, when we are able to put back that which we have to take out in order to make the mental picture of it, what we had to sever from the wholeness. When we look at a tree, we sever it from the wholeness of its true life. We can only understand the being of a tree, or anything, when we can put it in context again. That's not analytical, that's synthetical. So one part of anthroposophy is that it is intensely subjective.

And why can it be so subjective? Because even in our soul we carry, subjectively, the objectivity of the nature of the universe, within us. We have to have the courage, the moral strength to work in a subjective way: "It is I who do it," I who by understanding it makes the world whole again. The only way to make it whole again is by trusting that what lies deep in you is the truth of the universe. If not, we can stop learning, and people will tell us what is true and what to do. But that is not the future. The future is that each one of us, as Christof Wiechert said in the summer, has to become a little Rudolf Steiner.

That means to take as an example what he did, to do the research, to work on everything that you experience in life, even the most mundane things, to understand what I am doing. Because that's what the children do. They are just born, and they do the most amazing, mundane things over and over and over. Landing on their butt and getting up over and over. Trying to master the stairs over and over and over. What they are doing inside is trying to bring together, to understand deeply, to *research* what it means to bring form and to meet the outside world, through the senses, and to conquer that.

> *A participant had an interesting dream. A child had drawn pictures on her jumper. In reflection, it meant to her that we are all pictures drawn on each other's etheric bodies.*

Today we sang the song "How like an angel came I down." The picture that lies in the soul of the child, where he came from very freshly, that's always movement. The colors are alive, they move towards and away from you. The beings are alive and change all the time. When you sing, "How like an angel came I down," you touch the picture they carry in their soul. And then you might see that they go and draw a rainbow. The inner picture they carry of the colorfulness, the aliveness of the spirit world is reawakened by the words "How like an angel came I down/How bright are all things here!" There are so many more images in there. They reawaken for the child an experience. And then they might be able to either play it out or make a drawing. Or they speak about it. This is the process of reawakening the pictures that lie in the soul of the child.

The puppet play you do, the story you tell, the song you sing: these are tools to awaken in the child the pictures that lie in them.

What also lie in the soul of the child are the pictures for their destiny, their karma. And so it's not that the young child is already connected to their karma. That takes time, until the heart embodies all the pictures, and this little dwarf in the heart is able to see the pictures, the map. The moral pictures are in them, and this comes out in their play, too. They want to be a fireman, or a policeman. If you understand what a fireman or a policeman is, you start to see what kind of moral deed they want to do in the world. You have to understand that from the inside. That's what the world gives them as the garment for their inner moral impulses that will come out much later.

So let me talk a little bit more about the organ, the physiology of imagination. When we are one, two, three, all we are doing is building a body: maturing the body so that we can live in this body and find a home in the world, and learning to walk, to speak, and to think. These are tremendous achievements for a human being, that we cannot do out of our own inner drive alone. That is guided and guarded and helped and shepherded by the highest hierarchies, and by that being that goes always with humanity, that we call the Christ.

It's always worthwhile to think, why? Why can we not do it ourselves? Why is it the Christ that has to guard and guide us to be able to walk, talk, and think? Then there comes around two-and-a-half to three the time when the child feels "I am on my own." And this feeling of "I am now on my own" is accompanied by a feeling of loss and anger. What we call the terrible twos is a feeling of "I now have to do these things on my own." At the same time, wherever there is a loss there is a gain. There comes this feeling, "I'm not just on my own, I *am*." Which is tremendous too. With this "I am" and being left on our own in the world comes the ability to have memory.

Now we are right in the middle years: approximately three to five years, which we have made our focus of our conference this year. And you see already when you observe how a child grows that something starts to happen in their physical build. When you watch a very young child, you see that the head is guiding the formative development of the body. And you can actually see how slowly what is above moves into the child. Around three it starts to be guided not from the head, but there is something happening in the rhythmical system. The danger of crib death is past, because the rhythmical system, the breathing and the heart start to have their first maturity. It takes quite a while, until puberty, until they have really firmly established a rhythm that can sustain itself.

Until twelve years of age, there is still a very loose connection between the heart rhythm, the circulation, and the breathing. At twelve, that is—I wouldn't say fixed, but firmly connected. In the young child, the heart still goes with the emotions, the breathing goes with what is happening outside, and they are still separate from each other. But around three, you can actually start to see how with this realization "I am," (not as something they say, but something they feel) there comes an interest in the other. Because "I am," then "You are." This realization of the other is now a breathing process, or a periphery-center process, that means that if I can hold myself, I can also go out and experience the other. This is the basic social gesture.

So around two-and-a-half to three, there comes the new ability to be playful, to be in a different relationship with the other, not with the adult alone, but with the other child. And if you have something to add here, that would be perfect. Can you remember the transition in the child from "I am the most important thing" to when something new starts to come in?

> *From a three-year-old: an older child asked how old he was. He said, "I'm a little bit old, and a little bit new."*
>
> *Story of a child who has started to run away when it is time to put on slippers or dress to go outside. She was showing "I am going to do it my way!"*

When the rascal comes out, that is a form of social relationship too. "What if I do this? Let's see what she does!" It's a social gesture too, isn't it?

> *A participant's own child said, with a sucking in of breath, "Mummy, is you big?" "Yes, I am." "Is Daddy big too?"*

It's like an opening of eyes: there are other people here too!

> *A participant's youngest son went to daycare at age two. All the girls wanted to be princesses. He looked at her one day and said "Mama, you a princess."*

That is much more than recognizing boy/girl differences. You were shining. You were the queen! He just didn't know the word yet.

> *A participant's three-and-a-half year old son brought some silks and told her to put them around him. She put them around him like a shawl. He stepped back and said disgustedly, "Mama, this was when I was an old granny. I am a boy now!"*

I want to work a little bit more so that we understand the difference between reawakening the pictures that are lying in the child, and finding pictures that are seeds for the future. Also, I was asked if the work with pictures before birth and after death is different. It's the spiritual world, and the pictures are different, but the world is the same.

I will give you an example of how to find pictures, out of the grade school. You will help me to find what you do in the kindergarten using the same quality, but changing it. I'm talking about third or fourth grade, when the child is introduced to the animal world. Now when you introduce an animal, you do not make it into something else: "Oh, that's the heavenly cow that descends from..." That is not reality, and the children would not be able to go with it. But to describe the cow in a way that lets the child have a true imagination of what the child is, we can start with the stomach.

Describe how the cow becomes completely one with the grass. You observe it for hours and hours, and you see how it moves from one place of good grass to another, one with grass, with the meadow. How the whole apparatus of the mouth is constructed to be one with the grass. And how much grass or hay the cow has to eat to fill this *huge* space of stomach. The cow has four stomachs. The first is actually the biggest of all, and reaches all the way from the mouth to the rear end. The capacity for this first stomach is 120 liters. The capacity for all four stomachs is 200 liters. And after the cow has been one with the grass, when the grass is taken into the first stomach and she rests, she is still one with the grass, but now through bringing the grass up and ruminating. The cow has to bring up vast quantities of fluid in order to ruminate, to digest the grass.

When you describe in loving detail how the cow is in its complete being, it is a digestive being. It is not a thinking being, or a sensing being. It is an archetypal digestive being. So these are now imaginations that can be applied, when you understand that there are beings who live more in the digestion, in the metabolism.[1]

Now, by describing the cow, we can actually bring up characteristics of what it means to live in the metabolism. You can't be running around all the time. You need a lot of time to ruminate, to digest. So there is a kind of peacefulness. And then there comes the realization, "Oh, that's why in India the cow is sacred." Later, you can start to talk about why the cow is ruminating: what the cow is doing is to bring cosmic forces all the way down into the metabolism. That's why cow dung is so important for the earth.

These are imaginations that can rest as seeds for the future, in grade school, in high school, and for adults. But in kindergarten you will not describe the four stomachs. What can you do in kindergarten to make the archetype of this digestive being tangible, alive?

> *Story. Song. Gesture.*

Can you see the joy of a child when they see a picture book and experience the "Moo." *Moooooooo.* That's the whole cow. It's not even the story yet, it's the sound. If *you* have an understanding of the cow as this wonderful digestive being, in your sound of "Mooo," all your knowledge is actually living. Now you see the seed quality of the imagination you had when you understood the cow. This seed will bear fruit in your voice and in the way you pronounce the sound.

Sometimes we go too early into stories and songs, and do not use nursery rhymes. Nursery rhymes are wonderful carriers of seed imaginations. Often the story doesn't even match with what you want to bring; it's the sounds. How the children will enjoy doing the nursery rhymes over and over again! There you see the character of the rhythmical system and the breathing. It goes over and over and over again, until it is our own.

> *How do you come to the essence, the archetype of the animal? By meditation?*

---

[1] Recommended books for finding such animal imaginations are Rudolf Steiner, *Harmony of the Creative Word*, and Wolfgang Schad, *Man and Mammal*.

You study the animal, from a scientific perspective. Then you meditate. Anatomy is unbelievable in its many imaginations. We are the imagination of the gods. You can really meditate on anything in anatomy. That's what I mean by science. You need to know what is there. When I meditate on the spinal column, I know that there are five bones and seven bones, and that that lawfulness means something. Then you can find the truth of it. You need to be scientists too. You need to be everything.

Do you start to feel the difference between the pictures that come from the past and the ones that lead into the future?

> *What about being the cow? We do that in the circle.*

Absolutely. There are very few children who choose the cow. They choose the cat, the dog. That would be interesting research: why?

> *A participant asks about how slow to speak a nursery rhyme. She has understood that it should not be too slow, because the children have a quicker breathing.*

You have to take the cue from the children. If you are too fast they get faster, if you are too slow, they get restless. You have to actually breathe with your children. That's when your heart makes a whole out of everything, and you start to know where you have to speed up or slow down.

More pictures will come this afternoon. Now *ruminate* on it.

> *Mooooooo!*

We have time left to talk about play. In play the child weaves together the future and the past, the inside and the outside. He brings up into the feeling body what lives down deep in the soul and in the etheric body. There is an excellent book with articles by Joan Almon, Christopher Clouder and others, called *All Work and No Play: How Educational Reforms Are Harming Our Preschoolers*. I think it is out of print; I got it from a used bookstore. It's a collection of essays on the vital role of play, and also what it means today that play is transferred from the home or classroom onto the screen of the computer. Parents misunderstand the importance of play by thinking that play is there so that we become smart. If we become smart when we play, it is not play. We become *human* when we play. Schiller even says "We are only human when we play." This is true all the way to old age. We are artists when we are playing.

So this is the time when I would like you to bring something of your classrooms: how the three-year-old plays, how the four-year-old plays, how the five-year-old plays. Then we will look together at the difference.

What kinds of playing are there? This is your very own domain, children's play.

> *A description of one group: three-year-olds are doing a lot of house play, playing out social dynamics, while four-year-olds are going more imaginative play, moving furniture, playing dress up and constructing the space. Five-year-olds have more complex ideas and finer details.*

So the younger ones are more mirroring what is happening in the world, while the older ones are doing more planning and pretending. Good.

> *A story from a school that has an organic farm with lambs and sheep: At lambing time in the spring, the children were able to see the births and also deaths. There was an urgency to play that experience. Five-year-old girls started playing giving birth, caring for babies, nursing. They told the "dads" that they should go into the kitchen and cook for them. This was played day after day after day.*

You see there something of the archetypal experience in the soul of birth, connected with something that was experienced outside. And they played over and over and over again until it was understood. Now if that is not possible to play out, can you imagine where it goes? Can you feel how what the children do with rocking the babies and caring for them, how that goes right into the rhythmical system? The child in doing that is actually strengthening the heart and rhythmical system. Beautiful.

> *Description of a year when there were many "Luke Skywalkers" in the classroom: lots of movement and jumping and crashes and bangs. Teachers tried to redirect this play with little success; it would always pop up somewhere else. One day there were two girls playing in a house and Luke Skywalker came and asked one of the girls to be Princess Leia. And very soon Princess Leia was feeding Luke Skywalker scrambled eggs, redirecting the play as the teachers had not been successful in doing.*

By entering into that space of play, one child made it possible for the other child to enter in too and forget about the mental picture of Luke Skywalker. So when you want to heal excesses in your kindergarten, what do you have to do to make that possible? You can't say "Don't do that" or "Stay outside." You actually have to start to be part of it, and not be afraid of what happens in play.

When you take play out of the kindergarten and put it into the therapy session, you have to be completely unafraid of what happens in play. The most outrageous things can happen, killings and beheadings and hangings, but you can stay with it. If you push it away, then you push it down again. It is paramount that these pictures come up and are played out.

Now this is sometimes not possible in the kindergarten, because the child lives so strongly in imitation that suddenly you will have all these killings and beheadings. But this is the art of the kindergarten teacher today, how to do that. Maybe you have to have this child come a little early and be just with you. You have to find ways that the pictures can come up, so they are not pushed down into the soul and stay there, undigestible. They come out then as destructiveness, impulse control disorder, and so on.

Children today are coming out of wars. There are children that come out of Iraq, from Hiroshima. You have to take that into account. They come from the spiritual world, yes, but with pictures from a previous lifetime. So if you have deep compassion for what this person may have been going through, you will hold the play in a different way, and give it enough space. It's a very serious thing, play.

> *A participant spoke of trying to impart to parents how important this play time is: the mood of play, a sense of awe and reverence. It's as if two or three people are dreaming together the same dream. We shouldn't enter it; they want privacy. If we do it correctly, they can't even recount to the parents what happened.*

Deep wisdom comes out of the kindergarten. Only when you are in the presence of play does it come out in this way.

> *An anecdote of three ages playing at the same time. Two four-year-old boys were wearing harnesses, being strong "lions" pulling a boat. A six-year-old was living in the lofty world of "princess" and a three-year-old was shadowing her. The six-year-old had been playing "eating candy"; she had had a guest over the night before, a diabetic girl. Everyone had rushed around the house looking for candy to balance her insulin, which made a deep impression on the six-year-old. All morning she had been thinking about what it meant to be diabetic and have candy. She climbed on the boat and the three-year-old climbed on too, following her.*
>
> *The girl looked off in the distance, sucking on her "candy," and said blissfully, "Two diabetic princesses, off on their train, being pulled by lions."*

So what comes in here now that is different, with the six-year-old? A lot of their own wishful thinking. It's not the reality of diabetes, it's the reality of *the wish to have candy*. It's now coming more and more at the end of kindergarten and the beginning of the grade school that the personality comes in, in a different way. That is a wonderful example of the six-year-old.

> *A participant sees that around six years old the children start to play out death. As the etheric body being born, that birth is experienced as a death. They play games of dying and bringing each other back to life.*

Isn't that interesting?

> *Description of the difference in movement at different ages. Three-year-olds will go to the kitchen play area and be very still; four-year-olds are often imitating animals; five- and six-year-olds are very much into movement. They hop on one foot, make a circle with the chairs, play tag, cooperative games. The big ones pull the little ones in wagons outside.*

So what do you see happening now? At the end of the kindergarten period, which we will talk about next year, the six-year-old is already taking hold of the limb system. When they can pull and push and finally jump rope, that is when they have incarnated all the way into the limb system. Now they can conquer the world in a different way. You see the difference with the middle period, which is completely in this dream state that was described before. Rudolf Steiner says that we are dreaming in our rhythmic system. We are awake in our senses, we are deeply asleep in our limb system, and we are dreaming in our rhythmic system. So you could say these middle years are "dreaming" years. Sometimes the children wake up out of the dream, and sometimes they go even deeper.

> *A participant asks about five-year-olds, particularly, who are talking about playing and gathering things, but never getting to the game. They are getting things together but then suddenly they want to go do something else, and then it starts over again. Does it have to do with the rapid growth in their body? By the time they are six, they seem to follow through more.*

That would fall under the category of "planning" play, even if they do not play it out. And this being able to plan something has to do with that now there are forces coming free that are head forces. But they are still very playfully experienced, not as concepts yet.

> *What about playing garbage? Taking everything in the room and making a pile?*

Now use your imaginative powers and penetrate this picture.

Letting go, digesting?

When it is between three and four, you look at the heart. The heart takes everything and collects it in one corner. Or the breath—collect the whole environment and bring it in. That's collecting. And dumping? There the rhythmical system dives into the metabolism and dumps, so that we can take something new in. You see how in the play we have not only the pictures playing out, but the whole physiology played out.

Birth of the Imagination
PART III

This afternoon I think it would be right to think about whether we have in our knapsacks the seeds, the imaginations, that we need to go back to our homes. So I want to give enough time for questions, but first I would sum up with a few words by Rudolf Steiner, who is a master of imagination. Anthroposophy is not a philosophy that is out there. Anthroposophy is in each one of us. Steiner has given so much that we have enough to do for the next few incarnations.

Remember that yesterday we were talking about the middle sphere, the rhythmical system and the breathing that is now in the second part of the first seven years coming into its first maturity. In Lecture Eleven of *Study of Man*, Steiner says "in the chest, things are very different from in the head. From birth, from the very beginning, the chest has physical and soul characteristics. Unlike the head, the chest does not have only physical characteristics. The chest has physical and soul characteristics, and only the spirit exists in a dreaming state outside it. When we observe children during the first years of life, we must focus upon the greater awareness, the greater liveliness of the chest aspect, compared with the head aspect." This is connected to what you observe when you watch the children play. There you see the liveliness of the chest aspect.

So that's one thing. And here is another, again to remind us of the seriousness of our work, how incredibly important it is that we understand the anthroposophy of the child. We know about the anthropology of the child, but we have to go deeper. Anthroposophy means the knowledge, the Sophia, of the human being—no more, no less. So the anthroposophy of the human being, the knowledge of the human being, the study of man: that is what anthroposophy is. The importance of knowing about it as early as possible is really a heavy responsibility sometimes for you.

Here is a quote from Rudolf Steiner's later lectures, where he talks about the intense necessity to renew the social system. That was in 1920, and here we are in 2010, and not only have we not been able to find the three spheres of the social realm—the free spiritual sphere, the interconnected rights sphere, and the brotherhood or sisterhood in our economics, we are far from it. All three forms are becoming more and more mixed up. I can only hope that it will become so bad that it will explode and something else will come.

So in 1920, in these lectures that were given for the renewal of the social sphere, Steiner said,

> *The child is confronted today with something devoid of a pictorial element; the young person, on the other hand, possesses forces in his body—naturally, I am referring to the soul when I am now speaking of "body," for after all, we also speak of the "astral body"—forces seated in his body that will burst out elsewhere if they are not brought to the surface in pictorial representation. What will be the result of modern mistaken education? These forces do not become lost; they spread out, gain existential ground, and invade the thoughts, feelings and impulses of the will after all. And what kind of people will come into being from that? They will be rebels, revolutionaries, dissatisfied people; people who do not know what they want, because they want something that one cannot know. This is because they want something that is incompatible with any possible social order; something that they only picture to themselves, that should have entered their fantasy but did not; instead, it entered into their agitated social activities.*
>
> *Therefore, we can say that people who, in an occult sense, do not have honest intentions in regard to their fellowmen, do not have the courage to admit to themselves: "If the world is in a state of revolt today, it is really heaven that is revolting." It means the heaven that is held back in the souls of men, which then comes to the fore, not in its own form, but in its opposite—in strife and bloodshed instead of imaginations* (from *Spiritual Science as a Foundation for Social Forms*, Lecture 16).

So you see today strife and discord instead of imaginations. You see that it is a dire place we are in. It's the revolt of Heaven, not a revolt of the Earth.

It's a revolt of the Heaven that cannot relieve itself in the imagination in us. So it becomes like a cancer, eating up, destroying.

We look at illness as if it's something we have to eradicate, that we have to rip out and destroy, as if that is a war too. But illnesses need to be recognized, like any other being, in order to be healed. So I would like to leave this picture with you, the revolt of Heaven that comes out as strife.

I would like to take time for your questions so that we can digest all the concepts, the imaginations and pictures that you have been given.

> *A participant spoke about a boy in a mixed-age preschool, a young four-year-old. Ever since he was a baby, he would scream and cry so much that his mother recoiled. She related that when strangers would come up to him as a baby and say "Oh, how cute," he would immediately begin to scream. What kind of mental pictures has he brought with him? He has tantrums when he doesn't get his way, then flops down and can't use his limbs. The parents are also getting divorced now. He is a very strong, physical boy.*
>
> *Another participant responded: He needed to be nurtured and supported early on; the life sense is weak. Your meditative life with that child is very important. How you picture him and see him coming towards you is powerful.*

When you look at a child and say "Oh, what a lovely child," and he starts to scream, he actually has a large spirit/soul body that is not completely within the body. And if that is not supported by the parents, that the body can hold the life sense, as was mentioned, is too weak. It is actually agitated all the time. The child is not fitting in the body, because such a huge soul/spirit came. He is actually outside the body. By the way, Rudolf Steiner screamed for a whole year. And his mother carried him around the house for hours, day and night. He was a huge soul that didn't fit in a small body.

If the child is so perceptive outside of the body, he is extremely sensitive to what is around. That is why the meditative life of the adult is paramount. You work with the mother to understand that what she says and what she thinks he actually perceives. If it is difficult for her to change, then not judging her, but showing your love and compassion for the child can show her another way.

Steiner says in *The Education of the Child*, don't worry about the children who are loud and screaming and wiggly and don't want to do what you want them to do. They are fine. They have a lively spirit. The ones who are impossible in your kindergarten, they are fine. The ones who are quiet will have a hard time to overcome their inherited body. So help them to get alive inside so they get a little naughty. Naughtiness is important.

> *A question about four-year-old girls who were quietly playing in the house corner, and everything seemed fine. The teacher listened to their play, and found they were chopping up babies and eating them.*

There comes a play like this, and we recoil. What do you think about that? Lovely little girls who are chopping up babies. What is happening?

> *They are expressing their experience? They are feeling fragmented, everything is coming towards them?*

You can always be sure that what they play is what they experience. So while we can think that they must have been cannibals in the last life, and must have done something horrible, actually it is what they experience: a kind of fragmentation. Sometimes the play is not so nice, because the experience is not so nice. But what do you do? Protect this little house so that nobody will listen? How can you help these children who feel a sense of fragmentation?

> *A participant responds: I might say "Oh, I'm pretty sure the fairy mother might not have given us the little ones if she thought we might be cooking them." Or "Here are some nuts, you can use these." Not that I would want to stifle their play, but maybe they also see that I am holding a place for the healing deed.*

> *Another suggestion: With this fragmentation picture, the whole picture of how we have worked with images needs to be looked at. Have we given them trust in the human being? We need to make a greater impression on them than the fragmented life. So we revisit the archetypal activities of the human being, so that they can see this upright, lawful activity in their midst. The pictures that they have brought with them can meet pictures from the future, of what the human being is capable of.*

My answer would be is that the archetypal picture of the baby that has been ripped into pieces is the myth of Isis and Osiris, which is a picture of the heart. How old are the children? At age four, they are actually coming into the heart and the lungs. The imaginative picture behind the lungs is that of Isis, and behind the ribcage that has been fragmented is Osiris. And the heart has been ripped and fragmented in perceiving the world, which is damaging everything all the time. In Egyptian mythology there is this story of Isis and Osiris and Horus. Osiris for the ribcage, Isis for the lungs, the nurturing, holding of the lungs, and as if in a cradle, the heart. The heart, which comes into the perceptive mood in the years between three and five, perceives the fragmentation of the outside world that you have mentioned. So these children are actually playing their physiology.

What an incredible thing. And now you can help them to overcome this fragmentation, through the way you do your circle that you do every day or twice or three times a week. The circle is actually the picture of an unfragmented periphery for the heart. That's why you do circles. So if the children perceive something that is a periphery to themselves, a safe sphere, that is an unfragmented sphere for the heart.

> *Another comment: they are eating the pieces: that seems to be the resolution, the transformation.*

They send these forces into the digestive system. Isn't that fascinating?

> *A participant sees children stuck for days playing out something. Can they really transform all images? Or there other activities needed?*

No, that's why the understanding of the human being needs to be there. You can't just leave the children alone and think they will transform it. You have to bring the reality back, because in this digestion of pictures, you can get lost in the pictures. And then you lose the connection with reality. The teacher needs to be there, even if only in thinking, in understanding. It doesn't have to mean interfering with the play, but sometimes giving it a different direction.

> *Her impulse was to give limb activity, like sanding, before returning to the play, which seemed like an interruption, yet seemed to help it move through.*

This is such a good question, because with all healing you actually have to move into their process and understand it, in order to lead it out of the rut. You are approaching what is happening, but then leading it into another form. It's like when you are confronted with a person with an illness. That's homeopathy. In homeopathy, you understand the illness picture, and then what is making it fixed is also what will lead you out of it. You need to be the homeopathic remedy.

> *Another participant asks: do you understand through meditation, or while it is going on?*

Sometimes you understand it in the moment. You have to trust your intuition.

Another comment: A child was playing "garbage," but with glass and metal and possibly destructive materials and getting others involved. The teacher said, "It looks like there must be garbage in there, now it must be time to recycle." Then they got excited to transform it into recycling, with all sorts of inventions. An example of going with them, but putting them in the right road.

Wonderful. That's a good note to stop on.

Birth of the Etheric
PART I

We started this series of conferences in Eugene with the first three years of life, and then we talked last year on Whidbey Island about the middle years, which were about playing, and these very different kinds of playing. And now with the older child we move a little bit closer to what it means to be almost a little bit like us. There is a sadness in becoming a little bit like us, because the child now learns to recognize the world and think about the world in a different way. And I hope that through all that we do this weekend we come to an understanding of that painful place of becoming a little bit like "them." Because young children, the one- or two- or three-year-olds, they don't think about being like us. Their relationship to us is so purely love; they cannot help but imitate us.

Only in getting older do I begin to feel what a deep service, or love, imitation actually is. It's totally unselfish. And I start to get an inkling of why Rudolf Steiner says that the first three years of life—learning to walk, talk, and think—are under the guidance of the Christ. This is not meant to say that the Church has a hold on the development of the first three years. It doesn't. It's this complete acceptance of this place where we are—that is Christ. That makes it possible for the child to imitate in utter acceptance of who we are. And today some children question that, whether we are worth imitating. Some children hold back a little bit. Not because they don't have enough love, but because they have doubts of whether the world is worthy of imitation, so they hold back.

And that is later called autism. It's one aspect of autism, that the children hold back in doubt of whether we are worthy of imitation.

So today and tomorrow, we want to look at the child who has to make the next step. It's almost as if when you look at the one-, two-, three-, even the four-year-old, you can still see the backdrop of our cosmic origins coming through. And then they have to make this step of moving a little bit closer to the planet and being more here. When this step has to happen, there is a lot of turmoil, and we will look at that. You as kindergarten teachers know so much more about that.

I had to go further back to find what I can bring that will nourish you, that will make you excited again about the background of Waldorf education. I came back to the one place where I get always nourished again, and that is reading Rudolf Steiner. Rudolf Steiner puts many of the things that are still incredibly modern today in somewhat embryonic form so that we can take them and develop them. They are not totally developed all the way to perfection.

He speaks over and over again about the same thing. He repeats it. Threefoldness, fourfoldness, sevenfoldness. Thinking, feeling, willing. If you work with these ideas over and over again, you see that he kept them embryonic, he held back so that we can turn them into something that is exactly right for our time. He's not old-fashioned. We can take what he gave and make it into something that is now for the twenty-first century. I do not know if you have the same feeling as I have, that for about the last couple of years the world is actually changing widely and rapidly and shaking us up a little bit. The old things will not do anymore, and we have to grasp things in a new way.

So our conferences might have to be different and we might have to speak differently; we might have to stand here and embarrass ourselves a little bit because we do not know it all yet. I say this to encourage you not to hold back because you are shy. I am actually shy too. Have the courage to take your imperfection and turn it into nourishment. It is our imperfections, not our perfections, that are for the future. When we are perfect at something, it's actually done, and then it has to be destroyed again. We can make our imperfection into something, and the child sees that we are working too.

There is a course that Rudolf Steiner gave—interestingly enough, not to early childhood teacher, not to teachers at all, but to doctors and priests. This was in 1924, in September, so these are some of the last lectures he gave. He stopped lecturing at Michaelmas in 1924 because he had fallen ill. In these lectures called *Pastoral Medicine*—recently they have been published again as *Broken Vessels*—Steiner speaks about early childhood in a beautiful way. He says, "When you see the young child, you actually see that this child embodies the sun," and that the first seven years are completely under the rulership of the sun. But it's not the sun from outside, it's the sun from inside. The etheric body, this elusive thing that we think we understand and never quite understand—this etheric body has actually at its center the sun. And with the sun as the center of this etheric body we are connected to everything on the planet. It shines and sparkles on the crystals and stones from outside; it gives life to plant and animal; it connects the animal world, the plant world, and the human world with the life of the universe. And this universal beingness is what the child brings. It is the embodiment of the sun in the first seven years.

And then after the first seven years, this sunniness starts to ooze out and become available for the earthly ability to think and have memory and to learn. The sunniness that is inside and helps to build up the organs and the physical body, then in a way goes out and is available to learn. The transition is not that one phase stops and the other begins; now what starts to hold sway is that the moon forces start to come in. The moon forces are very different forces from those of the sun. The sun shines on everything; it comes up every morning, it might be covered by clouds, but it is always there. The moon, though, has faces. The moon has personality. The full moon has a different personality from the new moon. The waning moon has a different personality than the waxing moon. The moon at the equator has a different personality than the moon in Alaska. So you see that the moon forces from inside, not from outside, start to shine. With the older child, around five, you will start to see what we call an "attitude." These are not sun forces, they are moon qualities. Now the moon forces will work inside and then come free around fourteen, at puberty.

There are different ways of looking at how these forces work. In the first seven years we call what is inside "ether body." We could liken that to the sun. Then what comes in with the moon forces is our astral body. And the astral body works in likes and dislikes, in sympathy and antipathy. In yes and no. "I don't like it—I want it." That kind of personality starts to show up around five, five-and-a-half, six. So knowing this background, one has again a different compassion for the child who starts to show opposition, and that needs a different kind of approach.

Here I would like to make a little pause. I always like to work with you. Did what I just said bring up anything you want to share?

> *A story of a mother who came in in tears. Her daughter had just turned five. She said, "My child was always so kind and now she says 'No, why should I.'" The parents were not prepared.*
>
> *Another participant talked about a picture in* Phases of Childhood *of a child around four and a quarter and an older child. The gaze of the child changes.*

When you go with this picture of how the sun moves through the sky and what the moon brings up in us, the moon is our inner light, our inner life. In the moonlight we invite poetry. We are not just "out there."

> *A story of how the children sang "Happy birthday" to a teacher on the initiative of an older six-year-old girl. She was totally surprised, had no idea what they were up to.*

That is so great. What do you think that was?

> *It was not the sun quality, which would have been open, which the teacher would have sensed. It was something inner.*

She could hold a secret. Yes.

> *A story of a child who is going to turn seven. She said, for her birthday celebration, "I want you to tell me the biggest gift came from the moon."*

I want to cover in these three lectures the change in memory and thinking, and I would like to cover together with you the whole question about first grade readiness, which has become a problem. Lots and lots of good work has been done on how to make it more objective. This morning, though, I would like to stay with this change of the sun forces to the moon forces, and make that a little bit more palpable.

When you look at the forces of the sun, they create life. Without the sun, we would not have life on the planet. Life is selfless and lives itself. And when you look at that, there is another quality in us that actually is selfless and that unites us over the whole globe, and that is thinking.

We might use our thinking for our selfish means, but thinking itself is selfless. So the quality of the sun—which shines on everything, which is the center of the quality of life that is held and formed by the etheric body, and also the quality of thinking—is universal. There is no race, there is no gender, there is no folk, that cannot grasp a concept. It doesn't matter where we come from, it doesn't matter how old we are, it doesn't matter what color of face we have; we can grasp a simple concept. We can grasp it as children learn to grasp it when they are two years old, when they learn to name. When they see a tree, and the concept arises out of the object itself, that's a tremendous achievement. They see something, and the concept arises.

Now, we have to pay for that. What the child pays in order to have the concept is that we are not in immediate connection to the life of the tree any more. In order to have a concept of an object, we have to let go of our immediate connection to the life. We have to put it at a distance, to objectify it. First we name it, and then the concept comes. The life of a thought dies into the thought of the thought. This is quite something.

The very young child is immediately connected to the life in everything. Even with an inanimate, man-made object like a chair, it is so connected to the life of the form that even the chair can have life. There the sun-like quality is untaintable.

In order to think and to have concepts, we have to very early put in forces of the moon. The moon mirrors the sun. Imagine if we would be completely out in a sunny world and not have any shadows. What kind of beings would we be? We need this moment of inwardness, of shadow, of mirroring, to come to ourselves, and not be completely spread out like a young child into the world. In order to conceptualize we have to bring a distance, a little bit of darkness, a bit of shadow. Mirroring is the moon quality. And then, we "kill" or subdue something of the life so that the concept can arise.

These steps in learning to think are somewhat painful. And each time when a step is made, to be able to do more subduing or deadening, the child goes through a trauma. That is the three-year change, and it's again the five-year change, because between five to six years of age this ability to subdue the life of the objects around is at its maximum in early childhood.

So this is painful. There is a saying in German: "When the teeth shake, the soul shakes too." This recognition, which is felt on a soul level, of letting go of something that is so alive and going into the ability to name an object and to think, but at the same time to deaden it in order to become free of it, is painful. And so some children don't want to do it. Some children want to stay sun-like.

We usually do not remember these steps in our childhood, these moments of having to let go of life and move deeper into a world where we have to let go of the immediate understanding of the spirit and see the outer surface of things. If you do have a memory of a time when you could feel that, please share it.

This quality of thinking that we acquire we have to pay for with life. We give away life. It's similar with memory. The memory of the young child just born is a memory of the intense life in the spiritual world. And sometimes when you are present at a birth, and you look in the eyes of a just-born child, you still see all that memory that we do not understand, because we have been separated from it. You see all that memory of another world that slowly, slowly has to be dimmed for us to be able to be free. We have to forget in order to be free.

The memory of the newborn child that comes from another place slowly has to be dimmed and disappear for us to have memory of our existence now. The ability to have memory changes, as you know. In the first three years memory is only ignited by the object or the person or the place. And it is dependent on these. You put something behind your back and it's gone, for the very young child. Out of sight, out of memory. The memory is totally dependent on the object and the place. It's actually place-memory. Every morning when you go with your children the same way on your nature walk, huge memories come when you reach a certain place, but they are connected with that place.

If for instance you ask "What did you eat yesterday?" or "What did you do in kindergarten?" they cannot answer. They are not secretive—they just have no clue. But sing three notes—I visited a school where this was done—and all the children will come to you. Their memory is triggered by sense impressions. And this memory by means of sense impressions or something that is rhythmically put in their life unfolds in an amazing way, and they know exactly what to do.

It's different with the five-and-a-half or six-year-old. What happens? The chair is not alive anymore. There is this moment of "I'm bored." What is happening? What has been outside—sunlight—now moves inside. The ability to have memory is now inside, as the beginning of imagination. That which was only triggered by sense impressions or objects or places in the beginning, is now something you can see moving inward. If they began to play something yesterday, can they continue it today? *Yes.* Can they do that when they are three? *No.* What do they do?

> *They would start over. They would come into the room and see a tunnel they built yesterday, and just look at it.*

So why is that? Why does the memory change?

Here you see again the life forces, the etheric forces that have been working on the physical body in the earlier years. These life forces connect us immediately with the world of pictures. The etheric body is full of pictures. And with these etheric forces coming through we have access to the pictures that unfold in us as imagination. So see the difference: in the three-year-old the life that is ignited by the object, as a kind of fantasy, comes from the feeling life in everything. For a three-year-old, the outside and the inside of an object are the same. The outside and the inside of an animal are the same. They are inseparable. Very young children feel the inside at the same time as they see the outside. Then outside and inside start to be separate. But looking at the outside triggers imagination.

If you go that path, you see that it is the beginning of freedom. Because you cannot change when you look at something and it is immediately connected with your life. You are not free. You can experience this when you are ill, when you have a high fever as an adult, or you have a psychosis. You look at something and the inside and the outside are not separate any more. You think, "I am crazy, I am not free." There is compulsion, obsessiveness. In obsessiveness or compulsion, the life of the object is not subdued. It is still completely connected to my own life and it overpowers me.

There are children who cannot make this step properly of separating the life of the world from their own inner life. They are compelled to do something over and over again. That is obsessive-compulsive behavior. Or you have children who for whatever reason are impeded in the development of the ego, as immature as it still is. When the ego is not strong enough, as with handicapped children, then the life will never be separated from the object itself.

Now you understand why young children are afraid. If there is life all around, there is danger, there are fears. You find the same kind of fears in adults who are not able to separate the world from their inner life. This is a very important step, and you see again between five and five-and-a-half that the children bury themselves in mother's apron because the world is fearful and they cannot separate.

Could you help me with an example from your kindergarten?

> *A participant had a little girl in class, an only child who had a lot of adult conversation. While driving to school with her mom, she said "Mom, everything's changed. The trees have changed. You've changed, Mom. Even Harlequin the cat has changed."*
>
> *A nap-care teacher: A five-and-a-half-year-old starts crying "I miss*

> *my Mom"* as she is going to sleep. Holding her hand helps.
>
> Description of a six-year-old boy with fears, who wants to do what other children are doing and take things they are using; he actually was diagnosed recently with mild obsessive-compulsive disorder.

We come together in these weekends to know why these things are, and not just label them. The labels do not actually help us much. But *why* are the children like this? That's our task, to really understand the archetypal gestures of the etheric body and the astral body, so that they do not become empty words, but that we understand. It's so helpful when we start to understand what is happening.

The etheric body, like the sun, tries to make everything one. The basic gesture of the etheric body is the circle. It's the ball. Like the universe, there is an invisible skin around it. In physics, now, there is the understanding that there is a force that goes out and a counterforce that comes in. There is something about the etheric body that tries to make it all one. So when children start to be able to make a circle, and then put a dot in it, it means that for the first time, for a little bit, these etheric forces come free. They could not make the circle otherwise. These forces come free in stages; we have looked at that in the last two years. Now we have to look at what forces come free around five-and-a-half to six-and-a-half. Because then when they are free, the child is ready for first grade.

The etheric forces not only come free in stages, they also embody in stages. It's not that there is a blob of ether forces and it's here or there; through the first seven years, we actually embody our etheric forces in different ways. Now hopefully you start to see the relation between reflexes, sensory integration, and the etheric body. We are not talking about something that is different from the mainstream. How do we integrate our understanding of the etheric body with what is happening in current research? That's important.

In the first year of life, it is through the sucking at the mother's breast, and learning to contract and then expand again in relaxation, that we actually are drinking in our own etheric body and anchoring it. Then with speaking, through the reflexes that have to be internalized and become movements in the larynx, the etheric forces are being anchored. And then in play, the etheric forces are anchoring, through moving on the floor and so on. It is paramount that the etheric body be anchored before we can let go of it. It has to be all the way in before we can let go.

If we understand what is happening, what sensory integration means is that we have to go through how the senses actually work down on our physical body, on our movement body; only when we have integrated our sensory impressions can we then feel free and move out again. That is what sensory integration is about.

And then there is the time when a six-year-old is able to move through the whole body and show that by being able to skip. We are only able to skip because we are able to negotiate gravity. The moment when the child has an arch in the foot means that the child's forces are able to negotiate gravity immediately and overcome it.

Why do we have an arch? Why are we able to skip? Why, when we test for first grade readiness, do we see if the child can stand on one foot? These are all things we need to ask. What are we doing? Why is it possible at five or six and not at three? These are the questions we need to understand, and not just check them off a list.

I had started with the relationship of the etheric body with the sun, which is in direct relationship with our ability to think. The world of the thought, the world of the ether, the world of life, are synonymous. So when young children, five-to-six-year-olds, are able to build an imagination of what they want to do now, when they are able to have a memory of what happened yesterday, and now go with this memory inwardly, what will happen?

> *You will build a capacity for the future. For them to be able to remember what they came to do.*

Do they think so far?

> *They live it. It's part of the process. So what they penetrate at this point is laying the foundation for the imagery that they can recover.*

So what is the feeling inside the child when this capacity, this new capacity for a new freedom, is internalized? And when the moon forces of personality shine in?

> *They get quite bossy. They want to control what they create and tell others "Now you do this." It's a strength they have at that point. That's what my older children love to do.*

Are they a problem?

> *Challenging.*

They have personality, right?

Cradle of a Healthy Life: Birth of the Etheric • **91**

> *They can come in like a sledgehammer; they see themselves and their destiny in this new way, and sometimes it's not easy for them. It's an incarnating moment.*

With the child where it is difficult, there are two ways of looking at it, and two ways of helping. Sometimes there are children with a big destiny, "big" people who find in this transition that they do not know what to do with all that unconscious weight of the destiny that they have to meet. On the other side, you will see children whose body has not been made into their own, for whatever reason. The body gives resistance to that which wants to happen.

You know the body is what we have inherited. The first seven years are there to make this body our own, to overcome the inherited forces so that this new ability, this new capacity finds the vessel, and that we do not pour new wine in old flasks. There will be more difficulty if there is a very vibrant new wine, and there is a very old flask. So this is how we can help, by asking do I see the one, or do I see the other.

When you look at children who have been adopted, around this time there is almost a memory of their being adopted, much as they are loved by their parents. And so the anger is more violent than in other children. I have seen it over and over again. It's not something they carry in their conscious memory; it's a kind of bodily memory. With the sun forces that accept everything and shine down, and the moon forces of personality, deeply unconsciously coming in, there is also a kind of foreshadowing of the destiny to come, which again makes the children shaky.

So for today, there are these large overriding principles that I would like to put forth before we go into how to work with them. You see that what is happening right in front of your eyes is the mystery, the drama of incarnation. Today children are coming who meet a lot of pictures they have to digest. It's not just the farm, the tree, the cow any more. They meet a lot of pictures they have to digest and work through, and not get attached to. Even these pictures, these objects, will be imbued with life for the young child. They have to withdraw their life from many, many more things than ever before. And at the same time, it's made much harder for them because for their finer bodies, there are more subtle energies in our etheric space that keep them attached.

You see that from both sides the children have more difficulties. On the one side they have to overcome, to subdue the life in the objects, to make the pictures not frightening and alive; and on the other hand to not get caught in the finer energies. I'm talking about cell phone towers and things like that. They are real. We have a different electro-magnetic field than we did a hundred years ago. And all that is our life today. It's not that we have to shrink away from it, but we have to find out how to deal with it.

Birth of the Etheric
PART II

I would like to work a little bit more tonight to make more tangible what this etheric body is, what are these etheric forces that are born or freed when the child is ready for first grade. It is important that we have a good understanding of them.

If you doubt the relationship between thinking and etheric forces, just look at yourselves now, after you have eaten. Because the etheric forces are now working in the metabolism, digesting the food, and you are a little different than after you were this morning when you had just drunk a cup of coffee. Etheric forces are substance and form at the same time. It is hard to understand. It's a substance that in its quality has formative abilities. And there are four kinds of forming that might make it a little bit easier to understand.

There is a dimension that is like no dimension, and that is where the warmth lives. Soul warmth, or any warmth, is actually all over, and cannot be pinned down into a dimension.

Then there is the forming that has the shape of a radius. It is, so to speak, one-dimensional. That is the shape of light, that makes everything into an arrow, that comes from above to below. It makes very clear forms. That is the ability of the light ether, and the dimension is one-dimensional.

And there is a form of ether that forms the planes, so that it has in itself the formative force of making everything two-dimensional. You could say that is the quality of water. The element that is related to it is water, making two-dimensional planes. But then when you put water into movement, when moves, it makes rhythmical waves. You could say everything that makes waves is in contraction and expansion. You can actually hear it; it's a musical ether. And this musical ether is also working in the chemistry of our body. Nothing in our body is static. Everything is in constant expansion and contraction. And in our cells, we can only see then when they are in contraction. When they expand again, we cannot see them. So this contraction and expansion sounds like music, and builds two-dimensional space.

And then there is the last of the ethers, which is the most difficult for us to understand. We can sing and we can understand the musical ether. We can look at light; we can look at water. But the one that is the deepest, hidden in the world, is the life ether. And the life ether is where things are firm, where we have firm substance. The life ether makes the bones hold together. That which is most lifeless, has the quality of the life ether most inherent. And then you find in the bone itself, deeply hidden inside, the life where it works to build blood cells in the bone marrow.

It's the life ether that creates the three-dimensional space, that creates the form that makes us physical. The space we are standing in, that's actually life ether. That which has the highest potential for life is the most deeply hidden, so when we work with the atom, with nuclear energy, the nuclear energy actually forces the life out of the life ether, violently. That's why it's so huge. Nuclear fission is forcing the life out of what is actually still protected from our greed. It's tremendous energies that are deeply asleep in the crystals and in the earth.

So this ether body is represented in the rest of the universe in light, in warmth, in chemistry or sound, and in life. In our body, it is represented in a different way.

A colleague asked me, "Why do you say that the thought is selfless? The way we use thoughts is very selfish, it's self-centered."

Now you can understand that the ether-substance is not the content of the thought; it's like the smoke, and you speak something into the smoke, it gives it a form and this form comes closer to the thought. We could speak into the smoke and there appears a form. The smoke is selfless. But what we speak, what we put into the smoke, contains something of our selfishness. So the ether body, the ether substance, gives a selfless medium for the thought to be there.

The thought is a spiritual entity. Only in our world, in the physical body, in our three-dimensional physical body does the thought become something that has given away its life, its will, so that we can think it. And while we think it, we do not create what we think. Can you imagine? If the life would still be in the thought, then what you think would be immediately present. Can you imagine what a mess we would create?

In the young child the thought, which you could say is a God-thought, is still creating organs, is creating the child. There you see the thought is still alive, and slowly has to become devoid of life so that when we are six or seven we can think thoughts without creating a reality around us.

There is a transitional period when the child creates the reality around himself or herself. We do not see it, but for them it is life, because their thinking still carries that aliveness, that magic.

There you start to see the difference between thought and *thought*. The thought is a spiritual being; you could also say will. And in the spiritual world the thinking and the feeling and the willing form one being. In our world, we have to take it apart. The thought is the most dead, so that we can think it; we are dreaming in our feeling; in our will we are creating all the time, new realities. Our task as human beings is to make our thinking so alive again that we create, but in a moral way, so that we do not create specters and monsters and dangerous things—which in a way, we do. Out of our materialistic thoughts we create machines that give body to our thinking.

You see what actually happens in the child. What is magical in the first three years—the thought still creates the body—it needs to subdue. The ether body needs to separate from the child so that the child becomes conscious. And now you can understand that some children hesitate to become conscious. They don't want to have their etheric body free in the thinking. They still want to have it magic. But the danger is that if it stays magic, it becomes an illness. There is a time for magic, and there is a time for reality.

What we try to do in early childhood education is see that the reality and the magic of our story are congruent, so that the substances we use, the stories that we tell, the beings we create, have a direct relationship to reality. If not, it becomes separate, and the child with magical thinking begins to build magical beings that take him away from the world. They keep him from feeling good. They are threatening, fearful. They can be the stuff of nightmares, and later of mental illness.

So there is a time for fantasy, and there is a time for thinking. There is a lawful progression from fantasy, through imagination, to thinking.

In the grade school, images, imagination, imbue the thought again with life. Some children in the first grade do not want to let the picture die into the letter. They hesitate to learn to write and read for a long time, because they do not want to see in these two sticks with another stick through the middle an A. That's why in first grade one uses the picture to ease the way into reading.

If you understand that, it's not a contradiction that the ether body is the foundation for thinking, and at the same time the thought has to be devoid of life. It's just two sides of the coin.

I wanted to open up for questions for a few minutes.

> *A participant has noticed times in herself where she connected to the living beings, through a story, or someone she met; then later, sharing the experience with someone else, she could not put it into words, could not share it. What is that? Is it something to overcome? There is a resistance to killing the living thing to put it into words; but then one does not have the ability to communicate.*

That is so interesting, isn't it? When you go back into childhood, you might find that you had a tendency to be a cosmic child and not an earthly child. As a cosmic child, you would live more in the cosmic origins and be very connected to stories, but would hesitate to go into the place where the cosmic life would have to be subdued or killed into more academic learning.

If you would then follow the cosmic origins of our language, you would find that in the beginning there were no words for what we experienced. We were totally part of what happened in the cosmos, but it was a deeply dreaming consciousness. And then slowly, slowly, we had to let go of that and move into more of a picture thinking. In this later time, but still in the beginning of humanity, speech and music were still connected. Human beings did not speak yet; they were singing, they were sounding what they experienced inside. Out of that sounding, you find that in many cultures what needed to be told was put into a rhythmical, back-and-forth singing—the *Kalevala* is an example. In early childhood you have that around three, three-and-a-half, when the children repeat things over and over, and they love the nursery rhymes that go back and forth, back and forth. There is a memory of that time there. Speech came into being much later.

So that's one thing, how we express what we experience. There is something in you that hesitates to be quite earthly, and that may be why the children love you. They see that you maintain something that they still know. Do you need to change it? Only if you use your rhythmical sense. Singing would be good, and storytelling would be good. And have patience and accept who you are; it's very special.

> Question: why do some of us hesitate and others don't?

We choose our constitution according to our karma. It's a different life for someone who is more practical, and knows how to navigate the world; this belongs to your karma. Our constitution we actually decide together with our contemporaries. That would be another story. Now we talk about the child coming into life, but that is a decision we made when we fashioned our physical body, which is a spiritual blueprint. This physical body we fashion together with our students-to-be, with our teachers-to-be. So you changed the life of your teachers by being who you are. You changed the life of your students. It has implications, the choice of what constitution we have, implications for how we live in the world. At least that is my understanding.

> Should we interfere when we see children who are not organized, can't clean up, are completely distractible? Do I have a right to help the child move out of that?

Yes, you do. But the interesting thing is that everything in teaching, as in healing, as in parenting, is a matter of balance. It's actually a musical problem. When you hear someone is out of tune or out of balance, your inner sense of equilibrium wants to help to balance what is out of balance. That means that you first have to go where the child is. You cannot just put something here and balance the child. You actually have to go and listen to the tune of the child, to put it in a musical way, and out of that listening you will hear what can get them out of that one-sidedness.

That sounds a bit lofty, but it actually isn't. It's the same in healing, that you listen to where your patient is. But you don't get lost, you don't get in a state. You actually get the imagination or intuition of what to do, and then you balance. That's education. That's the will to heal.

See, that's what I meant earlier: when you are in this world midnight hour and you say "I will be a cosmic child," then your teacher is around and you say, "and you will help me. I will meet you again, and you will help me to get out of that state." And the teacher says, "Yes, I will be there."

> How does trauma or disruptive home life affect the child's etheric?

Good question. Remember that the etheric body is a kind of selflessness that cannot help but record. It's like the world recorder; it faithfully records everything by being imprinted by everything that is around. And in order to find the equilibrium that can build healthy organs, there needs to be a kind of rhythmical lawfulness around. It's not that everything needs to be in order. If everything is too constrictive, it's not good either. The etheric body is movement, forming, and substance at the same time.

You can answer your own question: a home life that is chaotic and disruptive is not helpful for the etheric body. And since children need to balance it out, if their environment does not balance it, what they need to pull in is their own astral body and ego. So they get a little bit too awake. In a sea of etheric forces that are in tune, they are deeply dreaming. They are awake, but they are dreaming because these higher forces, the feeling body and the ego, are not yet needed to keep the world in order. They can trust, "I know the world is a good place." They don't have to worry about it.

So a home life that is not rhythmical, that is not supportive, is able to make a child ill. That's one thing. But there is something that can actually counter that disruptive home life, and that is a mother and father, or caregivers, who in spite of what is around, give the child the sense that "I see you, I love you, I accept you the way you are." In the first years, what flows between the caregiver and child in this way will counteract what is in the environment, even the effects of war. One has to look at both.

The rhythmic home life is not the answer if there is not enough acceptance and love too. Rhythm without this acceptance becomes an empty shell. Both are needed.

> *They would need to draw in the astral and ego then too? If there is not enough warmth?*

The child tries to balance out the coldness. A child cannot help but love, so if something is love-less in the environment, the child will always put it on himself. "It must be my fault. I have to work harder. I have to flow out more. I have to adjust to Mom or Dad's expectations." This makes warps in the etheric that come out much later. That's why we go to counseling when we are forty years old.

> *A question about growing down and maturing up. Are they etheric forces? How does that fit in?*

This is about the idea that we are born from above to below and we mature from below up. How does that show? How do you see that?

> *Those forces have been described as etheric forces, as astral forces, or even as ego forces. It's confusing.*

I will try to come back to that tomorrow.

> *A question about how some of the children hold back and some take on the world. Some of the child's karma is the parents. Is it the child holding back, or is it the parent? Where do we see the child and where do we see the home environment?*

I will address that later too.

> *A participant had formerly understood that we were asleep in the will, not conscious of our digestion, etc. She was confused by something said earlier about the thought being will.*

Correct, we are deeply unconscious in our will. There the thought is still life. And the thought in the thought is the mirror picture; it is not life any more. The thought in the will—you could call it thought, you could call it memory—this spiritual thing in the will is deeply unconscious.

So, we will go on to what I wanted to bring today. Last night I thought it would be angels, but what came today was so different. I will talk about the teeth. It would be nice to talk about angels, but now we will talk about the teeth.

There are lectures Rudolf Steiner gave in Ilkley, in England in 1923, also quite late. They are translated as *A Modern Art of Education*. It is all about finding an understanding of the spirit in our time today. And he says in olden times, in ancient Greece—he was talking about the development of consciousness, in Europe you could say—it was happening in other places at the same time, but because Steiner was incarnated in Europe he took his examples out of the life where he lectured. If he had been incarnated in India, it would have been different. It's important for you to forgive me because I am European too. My limitations come from where I grew up; this is sitting in my etheric body.[1]

He says that in Greece, when one person looked at another, they saw in the physicality of the person they met the expression of soul and spirit. So

---

1 The next day, Dr. Steegmans further explained this statement: "Yesterday, I said something I want to correct. As a bit of an aside, I said I'm European, and it's just by chance that Steiner is European too. That's not true. I wanted to make it clear that our consciousness is able more and more to hold the whole earth. We are becoming more and more awake to the rest of the planet. We are conscious of what is happening in various places. *(Continues...)*

in the body, when you see these wonderful sculptures, you are seeing an expression of an ideal of soul and spirit. When they met another human being, they looked at this human being and it was as if they were transparent. They had a soul meeting, and understood how the soul and spirit worked in that human being.

That is not possible for us any more. In our times we have to find an understanding of the spiritual in the physical, but we cannot see it immediately any more. The reason is that in Greek times, way back, the soul development of the human being was still in the state of the feeling, of the sentient soul. The sentient soul is what we find in the young child. That which is around the child is felt all the way through the body. The sentient soul and the body are actually immediately connected.

You can see that when children are happy or sad. They have stomachaches, they feel it right through the body. You can see it in their countenance; you see how the relationship between what they experience and what they feel and express is immediate. That's sentient soul.

We are living as adults in what's called the consciousness soul. There we are removed from our body in a certain way. The consciousness soul is our first flower that opens to the spirit in such a way that spirit, in thought form still, moves into us. We can hold ten different opinions, and not have to react to any of them. We don't have to get angry, we don't have to beat

---

(Note continued) So when I talked about Europe, this cycle or epoch of cultural awakening in various parts of the world has happened before. It's like spirals. What happened in India, in Egypt, in middle Europe, then it will be in Russia, the Americas (the whole of the Americas, not just North America)—it's like a torch that goes around the globe, and somebody takes the lead, and the rest of the world follows. Even here in America, the materialism that rules the world actually comes from Europe. It's what lived in Europe that has taken over America, because what lived here before was not European.

So that we do not become culturally fixed, we actually should not be afraid to see that there are places on the earth that take the lead for the better or worse. When Steiner incarnated, he chose middle Europe, because that part of the earth carried the responsibility to help the consciousness soul and the ego as a carrier of the spirit into being. We failed, in a certain way, and it has to go underground again, but that was the reason. He had to be where the most light and the most shadow was. That was one reason.

The other was that he said the German language was pliable enough to express spiritual contents that are so hard to express. In the German language, you can make new words by just putting words together, and you can make endless words and they express something. In English, it's more confined; you say a word and that's what it is. So it's difficult to translate Steiner into English because it's more fixed.

So that's what I meant. It's not that there is a superior race, it's just that there is a place where the torch is and then it will be given on. Just to make that clear."

anyone up, because in the consciousness soul we are connected to our spiritual nature. In our spiritual nature, there is no contradiction between various impulses. Can you see the difference?

Today, we have to understand that the child is a spiritual being, and we have to meet it as a spiritual being. How do we do that? There is a lot of misunderstanding, because we think the spirit is something out there, unattainable, and we do not realize that spirit is in everything. No matter is without spirit, no spirit without matter. Everything that is materialized has a signature of the spirit, and today we have to be able to unlock the signature of the spirit.

That's why I want to talk tonight about the spirit, and how it expresses itself in the tooth.

With the older child in the kindergarten, we talk about the pushing out of the tooth—etheric forces come free in the child and now he is ready for first grade. We use these terms without quite understanding what they mean. We have to look at them rhythmically over and over again in every conference until we understand. I have to grapple with them over and over again.

You can take as a kind of motto these words by Rudolf Steiner, spoken in the second lecture of a series published as *Human Values in Education*:

> *Will we learn to contemplate every human life, every human being, with much more inner attention? And, because knowledge of the human being is instilled into our souls in this way, can't we deepen our love for humankind? And with this human love, doesn't our study of the human being give depth to the innermost sacred mystery of life, and with this love, won't we be able to truly enter the task of education because life itself has became sacred to us?*

That's the link to the child study. In the child study our observation skills have to be more and more accurate, because we fall so quickly into the soul nature of the child where we actually should keep our hands off. The child faithfully shows us his physical nature, and says "Here, this is my signature. You are free to read it, but when you touch my soul it's something that is private, it's mine." This task of reading the physical nature is really of our time. In this physical nature is the spirit, somewhat hidden.

So what about the teeth? Rudolf Steiner says that the same forces that push out the tooth when the child is six to seven, these forces are the same forces that are used for thinking.

Here we go again. How can we understand that thought forces are the same forces that push the tooth out of the gums? You have to turn yourself around and inside out. If somebody would have told me that when I was twenty-two years old in medical school I would have scoffed at him. You have to go and work in a way only artists can work, so that you use your creative, imaginative thinking from different points.

To understand this we would actually have to have some clay in our hands. We would form a ball, and then we would form an egg, and then we would hold the egg this way, and that way, and we would have an experience of the forces of gravity, having to do with physicality, and of the forces of levity, which have to do with the ether body.

It's hard to think it. These forces of gravity, which we have in common with everything physical, they make the tooth into a bone, the hardest bone in the body. The forces of levity, which have to do with our etheric forces, they push this tooth out of the gums.

Go with me again in your imagination. You have a ball in your hands, totally at rest in itself. It's like an egg before it's fertilized. And then you pull out a bit of that substance, and it looks like an egg. Now you put it with the round part at the top: what do you see, what do you feel? Then turn it around, with the heavy part at the bottom. Then your hands start to understand that this is the gravity of the earthly forces, and this is the levity of the etheric forces. These etheric forces, which are forces of levity, push out the tooth, and then become free for thinking.

Because we use these forces for thinking, we do not have another set of teeth. It's only because we think. If we would not think we would grow teeth, over and over again. But since we use them for thinking, that's it. We pay a little bit for our thinking.

Then you go a bit further. You look at the set of teeth in a child. It's very moving, very touching. With the child we talk about one quadrant of the jaws. The child has twenty teeth, that is, four sets of five. When we are adults we have four sets of eight, a total of thirty-two. So there is a change. The eighth set of four wisdom teeth, which is like the octave, is in our freedom. Some don't have them at all; some never will give birth to them. So the eighth set, we forget these. The others are quite lawful.

Therefore we have the number of five in the child, and seven in the adult. The change of teeth happens around age seven, and then around fourteen. It's incredible. When you look at the human being, at the spinal cord, you see that the five belongs to the lower pole, and the seven to the upper pole. We have seven vertebrae in the neck region, and we have five that are growing together in our pelvic region.

These are all gestures. You have to make your thinking alive and look at the gestures. When you look at the gesture of the upper pole, you see that in the upper pole everything tries to be closed. The head is closed, the thorax is closed. And in the lower pole, where the five reigns, everything is open. The ribs are open, the lower ribs don't even connect to the sternum, and in the pelvic area, the pelvis is not a head; it stays open.

Now you make the step to what you see in the teeth. The teeth of the child have an openness toward the world. When children are very young, they cannot close their mouths. It's a sign of readiness when the child is able to keep the mouth shut.

You see as a gesture in the young child an openness toward the world, even in the teeth. And then you see what kind of teeth they have. In each quadrant there are two incisors, one canine and two molars. If you know about the Man and Animal block in the grade school, there comes a times when the teacher talks about which animal lives more in the incisors, which more in the canines, and which more in the molars. Rodents gnaw, carnivores tear and swallow, the ruminant cow chews. You can see the awakeness of the rodent, the courage in the middle system of the carnivore, and the strength of the metabolic system in the ruminant, the cow. Very different gestures.

The child's first creation of a new tooth would normally be a molar again, but that has changed. A few years ago I talked about how first grade readiness has to do with the first molar that is coming in. Today, children actually are half and half. Some have the incisors; others have the molars first. So it is shifting from the metabolic pole to the thinking pole. Children are getting more and more awake in the upper pole.

So there is a shift now in humanity, showing itself in the teeth. When you go back a bit in history, in anthropology, you see that which teeth came first has changed tremendously. Right now we go from more resting in the metabolic pole, more into the appearance of the thinking pole.

I cannot answer all the questions because I do not have all the answers. I live with these questions. When I come together with colleagues who have been doing research into the teeth, what I come to is that these different times and different ages have to do with intense individuation. Individuation is not a sign of the ether body. Individuation has to do with the astral body taking hold of the etheric body. Moon, not sun. So the individuation is pushing more and more into the time of the sun forces.

Is this connected to girls getting their period earlier?

Yes.

What about growing extra teeth?

We actually have the possibility to grow teeth throughout our whole body. The growing of extra teeth is a sign that the etheric body is exuberant in building teeth. There are children who have teeth in other places too. Sometimes you have children who have a double set. They cannot let go before they make a new creation.

A participant is noticing more and more children who have teeth pulled because the new ones are coming in.

This is horrible and unnecessary. You override the formative forces of the body by using mechanical things to put them in a certain place. If we would be respectful, we would wait. Now, in some cases. we cannot wait because some children have jaws that are too narrow for all the teeth. I am not talking about that. But teeth are being pulled that would come out if you would do therapeutic eurythmy, or give homeopathic remedies. You have to work with the etheric forces, and not with the mechanical forces of gravity. Then there are teeth pulled that are an expression of soul and spirit.

More babies are induced in America than are born normally. If we can't wait for babies to be born, we won't be able to wait for their teeth.

That's right.

I wanted to show you how beautifully this expression of our soul/spirit is depicted in our teeth. In the child's teeth we have the number five. This is now the chemical ether, the musical ether that works with numbers. The fifth in music has a different feeling than the seven. The child lives in the mood of the fifth, down to their teeth.

With the seven coming in, there is a closedness to the world coming in. We close our mouth, we close off our teeth. Around ten, we go through the nine/ten-year change, which shows that in the soul/spirit we connect more deeply to the breathing system. It's not the stage we have at twelve, but around nine the child has the feeling "Oh, I have an inner life that is different than the outside world. I am actually different than the world outside." And there is this feeling that comes with the nine-year change of "I'm lonely."

At this time, when the rhythmical system starts to mature, there come two teeth that nobody has in the whole animal kingdom, and these are the premolars. They build a bridge, a kind of in-between, a new sound in the melody that has never been before.

They come in this time of the nine/ten-year change, which I always find so wonderful. And then at twelve there come the twelve-year molars, and then what is totally individual are the wisdom teeth, which may or may not come through. And you have to look at the individual: has this person used his thinking forces too early, or are they held back? I would not say, "Oh, you are a lazy person, or a stupid person." They are only called "wisdom" teeth because they come at a time when we already have some wisdom, not that they show that we are wise.

Don't feel bad if they do not come out. You can still get them to come out homeopathy and with therapeutic eurythmy, when you are older. With eurythmy you work with etheric forces. It all works together.

I see I am at the limit of what you can hold, or at my limit maybe. Are there questions about the teeth? Could you follow me? I could go into the form of the teeth, I could go into the substance of the teeth. With the substance of the teeth, there are also two poles. There is that which makes hard, closes off, comes from above. That comes from the iodine. There is that which gives substance; that comes from below, with the magnesium. So all these poles of metabolism and thinking, that which closes us off or makes us hard or kills things—this signature you find through the whole body, which is to me always a wonderful thing to see.

> *A question about a child who can't chew hard, is unable to bite a carrot.*

Usually their enamel is not strong enough, so you would say the forces that come from above, the hardening forces, are weak. You would have to look and see how to work with that. Sometimes a substance is missing in the food.

> *Does emotional instability in the child affect the teeth?*

What would you think? If these life forces that push up the teeth are compromised through emotional upheaval, would you say that that would also compromise the teeth? If we compromise one side, it shows on the other. It's a question of balance.

> *Does an instructor have a right to intercede if he or she sees something happening?*

You touch something that is so difficult to answer, because sometimes it depends a little bit on you and your karmic relationship to this family. By going into the family and doing the best you can, you interfere with something that could have been different. Are you willing to take the consequences? That's all. Not that you did something wrong, but are you willing to take the consequences.

With everything we do in education, we are changing something in the child's karma. Karma weaves itself all the time, every moment in you. So when you say "I go into the family, because I just need to do something," then that also has to do with you, and you have to question your motives before you do it. The ground rule is that the child has chosen this family, and first we have to understand why. This we can only do in our meditative work, or in asking ourselves, "Is it because *I* cannot stand it?" But if a child is beaten black and blue, do I stay home and say "It's the child's karma?" No! It's not even a matter of what's right or wrong, but of what is healthy and how you can balance it out. It's really a difficult question.

I'm in a healing profession, and I ask: do I do something about it, or do I wait? This question comes over and over again. I have to make sure that the bodily-soul-spirit integrity of the child is maintained. You might have to talk to the parents; that is the route to go first.

> *A question about a child who sucks his thumb, very far back in the mouth.*

Every touching of your self gives self-awareness. When you suck, it's even deeper self-awareness. In our mouth, we have three areas of awareness: the first is that we explore things, the second is that we feel things, and the third is that actually we touch deeper parts of ourselves that are usually unconscious. When a child goes very far back, it is touching something that really needs to stay unconscious.

In the swallowing part of our mouth, way back, we do not normally feel and we do not investigate any more. But in bulimia, for example, the consciousness in this part is maintained, as a means of feeling yourself.

Birth of the Etheric
PART III

I will start with anthroposophy and the *Study of Man*, to try to address the question about what comes from above and below. Is it etheric? Is it astral? Is it ego? How can we understand that?

These are the questions that Rudolf Steiner tries to address in one of the most difficult lecture cycles, which is the teacher's handbook, or the teacher's meditation book, that you can study to the end of your life, because it's so difficult to understand: *Study of Man*. And then a couple of years later, when Rudolf Steiner realized that these teachers he had trained so carefully in this first time when the Waldorf school was founded in 1919, that they still didn't quite get it, he gave another lecture cycle that is still incredibly difficult, and that is called *Balance in Teaching*. So between these two, maybe we can come to an understanding of which forces are streaming into us from which angle.

And so when you read it's the ether body, and then in another place it says the astral body, and then in another the ego—all three are right, but you have to see where we are when. And so without making it too complicated for you, I just want to tell you a little bit about what is happening from early childhood to when you are twenty-one.

In the child that you have in your care, from birth to seven years—and the seven-year cycles are only approximate, and they actually are getting less and less exact, but still I stay with the first seven-year period—in these first years of life, the spirit/soul, which is later carried in the astral body and ego, is still completely working inside. Spirit/soul is working in the child and creating him from inside out, creating the organs.

So spirit/soul, under the wings of the etheric body, moves into the newborn child, and is held like in a container and works from the inside out. In the first seven years, the ego forces are not free. They come free when we are eighteen, nineteen, twenty-one. Even if the child says "I," or has an attitude, or says "no" or is contrary, these are not ego forces that are free. That's important.

The feeling body, that's what we call the astral body. That's the carrier for the soul. It lives as a gesture in sympathy and antipathy, and also is not free in the child between birth and seven. It is also deeply hidden, and actually makes sure that sympathy and antipathy are physical. As physical forces, they help with breathing, they help the heart to beat. As physical forces they are contraction and expansion. These are freed when our teenager is around thirteen or fourteen. Then these feeling forces come free to be at their disposal.

The life forces, the etheric forces, which have to do with our growth, and are the carrier for what we worked on yesterday, thinking, memory, and mental pictures, are also not free in the young child. In the first seven years, this etheric body, which is our formative body, our life body, which we have in common with all the universe, is being freed in stages in the first seven years. Then around six or seven it comes free to be used for mental pictures, memory—a different kind of memory.

There is one place, when the child is born, where you see that the ether body is already free, and that is in the place of the "third eye" on the forehead. There is a little place where the etheric body of the child is free to search for the mother's face. In the movie *Babies*, there is this incredible image of a mother in Africa who is holding her baby, and they go forehead to forehead. And then you see some pictures of the Madonna and child, and they are connecting here. It's like a little light. Mother has it, while Father comes in later. I do not know how it comes about; I have not heard many people talk about it. But there is a little light and another little light and the child looks for mother's face and finds her.

You might remember it from when your own child was born. We think it's just the sucking reflex, but it actually isn't. There's a little piece of the etheric that looks for the other etheric.

And then in the course of the next seven years, the etheric comes free. We worked on that yesterday.

Now we have to make the next step, and look at the forces that stream in from above and below. When we are on the etheric plane—forget about the astral body and forget about the ego—on the etheric plane, what streams in from above are light ether and warmth ether, and what streams in from below, through the earth, are chemical ether and life ether. And there is no turmoil about that.

Now we are talking completely about ether. Light and warmth give us the warmth of thinking. Maybe you actually have a memory of that, how the world starts to light up, getting lighter and lighter. And from below comes the stream that helps us to mature what is born from above. The life and musical ether order what is born from above.

Now I'm going to the soul. The thinking forces are from above, and the will forces come from below. You see that we are free to think, to build pictures, and the forces that move our limbs come from below. We do not produce the will in ourselves.

So the task of the teacher—it's good to know as an early childhood teacher what is happening in the grade school—the task of the teacher is to harmonize the forces that come from above and the forces that come from below. You do that by addressing the feeling. Because at the end of this period, when the forces from above and below have done their work and come free, they come free as feelings. They live in the soul, in the astral body of the child. You see that in sixth, seventh, eighth grade, when there is poetry and deep, deep feeling. There is a little hint of that in the nine/ten-year change, when the child has this deep feeling of loneliness I mentioned yesterday.

Everything in the grade school needs to be taught through feeling. Through feeling it will take hold of the will, which is basically coming from the future, so it has to take hold of the will through feeling, and that will bring the consciousness forces in. We do not teach from above. We wake up the head forces through the limbs. That's the mantra. It's not that we do gymnastics so that we can think better; everything that is happening in the grade school has to be done with feeling, even physics and algebra. It's not that you are sentimental about it and make little hearts around whatever you do. It's that the children get so excited at whatever you bring, because there is truth in it. They get so excited that they cannot help but move their limbs.

It's a very different gesture from the head forces, because the head is the place in us where we need to be still. The head is the king and sits in a chariot and likes to be pulled around. Imagine if when we have to think we would have to nod our head all the time. We would get dizzy. So the head wants to be quiet, and if you gave the head the leadership over the rest of the body, the whole body would be quiet.

Now you see with children who are taught intellectually through the head, what happens when they finally get out of the classroom. They have to move, because you can imagine how it is when you have been held down all the time. And then they do not know what to do with their feelings. So teaching through the head will actually make children aggressive. Aggression comes when the feeling has not been ennobled. The feeling ennobles the will, and if the feeling cannot ennoble the will, it stays like in the young child.

In young children, the will is not ennobled either. The feeling is not free yet. What they see or experience or feel goes immediately into action. Two children are playing happily together and now one takes a shovel and bangs the other on the head.

As adults, we are threefold; we feel what we do. The young child doesn't feel it. It's dangerous, actually. How can we understand that there is an impulse that goes without feeling right into the will? How can we help the child to not do that?

It would be different in a second grader, or a fifth grader, right? Interesting. If you know what is underneath this, we will not give a lecture to the small child: "You do not do that." How can we make it an experience for the child? That their hands experience what they need to understand in their head? They need to experience, but not hear it.

The ears need to be connected to the feeling life. But if the feeling life is not free...

> *If it's healthier to not say it, do we just hold their hands and tell a story?*

No. You can hold the hand, and tell the hand. Sometimes you have to say "no," just to interrupt. But the younger child you can tell, "This hand has done something." Remember, with the very young child, the hand is like a separate entity. It has its own life.

So this was on the level of the feeling body, where the will and the thinking need to be ennobled by the feeling. If a child is for instance holding back by being too dreamy, and does not want to move yet, how do you act? I'm now talking about between seven and fourteen. You need to know if it's because they have such a tremendous force in their will that they try to hold it back. How can you help them to express themselves also in their will?

Then between fourteen and twenty-one, we often think that it's the thinking that wakes up. It actually isn't. Now we are all the way down with our ego, we are talking about the ego. Between fourteen and twenty-one, the ego body is able to hold us back, to hold us still. It is able to hold us upright, holding the equilibrium between all three dimensions of space, and to negotiate with the forces of gravity.

Remember I said that around seven the forces of gravity are overcome and the child is able to jump rope. Now it's a different kind of emancipation. The ego is able to totally move through the whole body from inside and out, and the young person is now able to walk in freedom to his or her karma. That is wonderfully depicted in the way we speak.

Yesterday evening we talked about teeth; everything is connected. The young children discover and conquer, when their thinking forces are free, the ability to speak tooth sounds. Before that it's the lips. Steiner said that when you look at a five-year-old use his lips, the whole organic forces are still in the lips. So when the formative forces come free in the thinking process, you are able to speak the T and the D. And when the feeling forces are free, the lip sounds are able to be expressed. When we look at a fourteen-year-old, you see that the lips can express feeling. Then between fourteen and twenty-one, it's the palate. Then you understand this strange thing. In puberty, when adolescents try to be cool, they actually talk in the back of their mouth. They do not want to show the rawness of their feelings by using their lips and their teeth. Or when the young person feels insecure, they make a clicking noise to calm down and have a kind of ego presence.

It's always amazing to me how these things that we talk about in a rather coarse way—ether body, astral, ego—how they show themselves all the time in the development of the child. So when you do a child study, you can look at how the child speaks. Where does the child live in speech?

What comes from below is the whole soul/spirit. But we take it apart in order to understand it. What comes from above is the whole soul/spirit. But in our head, we subdue the life part in order to be able to mirror and think. In the lower part, where we are the most human, we are deeply unconscious. You can meditate on that. You, who you are—Anne, or Wendy, or Mary—you live also in the will. It's an interesting meditation, because we always think that "Mary" is the one who is conscious. But "Mary" is also that which is unconscious, and that which is dreaming.

> *So from birth to seven the soul/spirit forces are coming in with the etheric from the top and the bottom?*

Yes.

> *And the forces of the astral body…*

They come too. But they build the body. They are coming in, but they are not free. The soul/spirit comes flowing in all the time. But in the young person it builds the body, then it builds the feeling, and then it builds the will. And then it is free on all levels.

> *Is it that the body is built by the etheric, and then the soul/spirit? Or the etheric is like a worker guided by the soul/spirit?*

There is no way that anything can build up our body as a human being other than the astral body and the ego, which are human. Imitation comes from that which is human in us, responding to what is human outside. If our human soul/spirit would not be present, we would not be able to recognize another humanness. We are human from the first moment of conception. First our ego and astral body are living outside in the sheaths, working in the sheaths together with the hierarchies, and then they slip in right before birth. And they are there working all the time, but then they come free. It's not an acquiring of these forces. They are all the time there, but it's a becoming free. That is so important to understand. The guidance is always from the human soul/spirit, our eternal ego. If you have got that, sometimes you can forget about what comes from below and what comes from above, because you remember—it's there.

> *But if it's just there, then what is coming in? Is it a constant streaming in and out?*

See, it's our predicament that we are so fixed. We cannot imagine that while we are in we are also out. We are as big as the whole universe. So we are streaming in, and then we are realized in this incarnation in a physical body. There will be other incarnations where we don't have to be so fixed any more. It is in order to be able to think and to be free that we are so fixed. We forget that we are actually connected—right now, standing here I am connected to all the planets. I am connected to all the soul/spirit out in the universe, not figuratively, but literally. That is so hard for us, because we are so dense.

> *An image from Rudolf Steiner's book* Psychosophy: *the stream of the future is coming on the astral stream; what comes from the past on the etheric; and where they overlap is the present moment*

> *that Christ holds for you, your consciousness now in this time.*

That is a good picture. You as early childhood teachers, you are working with your etheric for the healthy physicality of the children. Now, there is a danger, because the etheric comes from the past and is conservative. It tries to create the same things over and over again. It is formative forces that want to maintain the form. So there is a danger that kindergarten teachers are conservative and try to hold onto the same. You have to watch it. In every school there is a little skin around the kindergarten, and you have to watch it, because that's what you create for the child, that's the etheric, but as a colleague, you have to move out of your etheric and go into your ego.

So, you have to be conscious of that. Where am I? And as a movement, you can actually take the torch and bring anthroposophy into the future out of your ego being. But you cannot do it if you create the same over and over. You need to be movers and shakers!

Maybe one more thing: what comes from above comes directly, and what comes from below has to penetrate the earth. There is a different quality. What comes through our limbs is actually different from what comes from our head. In our head, that we are so proud of, we are the most similar to animals. In our limbs we are the most human. Can you believe it? Steiner says we can only understand it if you take a long bone and turn it inside out like a mitten, and then you will understand something of how the head is actually the metamorphosis of the limbs and vice versa.

So to make your thinking soul pliable and plastic, it's really difficult.

> *Is that because as you age your thinking becomes more and more hardened? Children are more flexible.*

It doesn't have to be. What happens is that the young child works with the etheric body all day, and in the evening it's really tired. But in the morning they wake up again and it's all restored from the night. They don't have wrinkles, they don't have old skin, because the etheric body is directly connected to the physical body. Aging happens because slowly the etheric body is separating from the physical body. By separating it is actually open again to spirituality, but you have to work on it. It doesn't just come.

Why you get wrinkles and all of that is because the physical body is slowly less and less penetrated by the youth forces of the etheric body, but now they are there to enable us to study. On the one hand the memory is getting weaker, but remember the memory has to do more with the antipathy forces. The ability to understand the world is getting more and more rounded. That's what I experience. The older I get, the more I understand. I might not retain it in the same way, but I understand more. So there is hope!

The interesting thing is these etheric forces, if they are not used in a constructive way, then cause old people to get bitter and gossipy and want to hurt other people. They have almost a type of clairvoyance, but they use it in the wrong way. If we don't open it up to the spirit, we open it up to hurt other people.

We don't have much time for first grade readiness, but that was important.

What are the signs of first grade readiness, we ask? With all our signs, we still have children in first grade who don't seem to be ready. What is it? I have made many mistakes in holding children back or putting them into first grade too early, and there is harm in both ways. If you have a child whose etheric forces are actually free to learn, but who is socially raw, what do you do? It appears that in first grade they cannot hold this space that should be open now to learn—remember, in the grade school we are working through the feelings into the limbs and then into the thinking. We can be mature in one way, and not another. What do we do?

> *They become angry or aggressive.*

It's really impossible to hold them in first grade. They act up, they do not want to hold the circle; they are bright, they can learn, but they cannot hold the environment. I don't have the answers, actually. I want to work with the questions. You know all the signs; it's not about that, it's about what if it doesn't happen properly. The checklist is three or pages long, and we still do not have yet the ability to always meet the needs. They can do all the things: skip, stand on one foot, and still there are questions.

> *A participant had a child who was disruptive and not imitating in kindergarten, but not ready for first grade either socially. She suggested that he repeat first grade.*

A child who is awake, doesn't imitate, but also doesn't recognize authority. That's what happens when imitation starts to cease: authority needs to be loved. If there is a child who does not accept either, what do we do? What do you see here?

> *Go back to the movement. They are often not in their limbs. That seems a good place to concentrate. Burrito wraps, rocking.*

Let's wait a little bit for solutions, while we gather the questions. What do you see?

> *Silliness instead of imitation, diving into the circle, not responding to redirection.*
>
> *Another comment: More and more children are coming into first grade who are not able to draw an archetypal person or house. They draw dot-dot-line-line pictures.*

This is an observation out of the remedial work. You are seeing first- and even second-grade children whose drawings are very immature. It's amazing how the drawings have changed. If you could hold them back till they can draw properly, you would have ten-year-olds in the first grade.

> *A girl with a March birthday was very attached to her mother; the mother requested that she stay in kindergarten another year. The child is messy and disorganized, never moving with the group or completing a task. Yet she has a March birthday.*

This ties in with what was asked before, about a child who is held back through the fear of the parents. So these stages of separation that don't happen because the parent is fearful of the world and so the child is held back because of that fear. How do we work with that?

There are so many questions that we could work on, but I would like to start there. When you realize that a child stays in chaos, is not able to order the world, then you know that this child still lives in the chaotic movement of a much younger child. Something has not penetrated: the ordering forces from above. They are not just thinking forces, they are also ordering forces. What often appears is that the ether body, instead of building up a healthy body, falls into bad habits. It is a bad habit, not being able to order the world around you. There is not a rhythmical introduction of the children at home to taking care of the space. You can do that with a two-year-old, through imitation. When this habit is not developed, that can be the foundation for a temperament that is out of balance, sanguine but almost pathologically so. Is it right to hold them back in kindergarten? First grade is about creating good habits. I don't think it helps to hold children back in kindergarten when they need to be in first grade.

About the drawing of children today: the children draw their inner experience of their body. These are archetypes of their inner experience of their body. So when children in first or second grade still draw disjointed stick figures, then they have not filled out their body with the life body. They actually feel their skeleton, almost.

When you look at the development of art, from the Greek figures to today, we actually have the stick figures now. That means something. We have come to a place where the ego that lives in the skeleton, in the bones, is raw. These children are actually awakened, the ego is not in the sheath any more. They are experiencing the world with the ego without having the ability to deal with it. That's why they cannot hold the circle, because the circle is way too painful. They cannot listen to a verse because it is too painful. They have to make it silly because they are raw in their feeling life. It's not that they do not feel; they are silly because they are so pious. That's what I have experienced. They have to harden their feeling body because they cannot deal with the intensity of feeling.

A child who is the jokester or the clown is always insecure. Always. They don't feel funny; they feel horrible.

> *A participant has a child like this, and in the birthday story when he comes to the gate of birth he makes a funny face every time; he doesn't want to hear it.*
>
> *Another participant asked: The ego is awakened, so the feelings are raw?*

The soul/spirit is raw. They are aware of the world in an unprotected way.

> *Like being premature?*

In a way. It's almost like being skinned. So if we hold them back and we help them to grow a skin in the kindergarten, that means they might have to skip a class, because they have to meet the class content that is true to their inner physiology. I've really seen that. I've held children back, because they seemed to be too raw, but then around fourth grade, after the nine/ten-year change, they became cynical, because they did not meet the content of the main lesson that was true to them. Waldorf education actually did not meet them any more, because the curriculum is so finely tuned to their inner development. We have to look at both things. The grade school and the early childhood, instead of being separate, have to work more and more together, and find ways of working together.

These children are actually creating new communities. We are not in the time of the ether body any more. We have our ego, to be creative.

> *Can children who struggle come for main lesson and then go home?*

It's often just not a possibility because both parents have to work. But I will take that up.

> *When children are held back, and then don't fit the curriculum, what is your experience with them skipping a grade? Can that be a solution?*

Yes, if you take that into account. See, fifty or forty years ago there was six days of school. Then people said "Oh, you will never be able to do the curriculum in five days." But we are able to do things in a shortened form, if we meet our children. That takes the creativity of the teachers. Teachers may be suffering the effects of bad teaching themselves and not be so flexible. The children are asking something of us that we may not be able to do. That's a dilemma.

> *A participant was heartened to hear that first grade was about good habits. In that mood, the first grade teacher is recognizing that first grade also belongs to the first seven years.*

You create the habits now in a different way. You move from imitation to authority.

I've just watched in one school, with a teacher who is going through his fourth if not the fifth cycle, how he had to take in and "massage" all the children who were thin-skinned, or a little bit old, and so on. I saw him dance every day and work so hard that after main lesson he was almost gray. And he is an experienced teacher. I saw what I took for granted, because I expected that a first grade teacher could take every child and eventually everybody would fit in. I saw in him that it was really hard work to be able to hold with your consciousness children who cannot follow, who throw themselves down or start to scream if something is too loud, who flail. And then to be there in every moment, it's really like a massage. So I don't think it's the solution to take everybody in first grade.

> *If you have a premature baby, there are ways to get it back on the right track. So with the etheric that comes too soon, what does it need? What can you do?*

What would you say? You work with the forces of warmth, rhythm, protecting the senses, and then you can actually move or internalize what is exposed too much. You can work with food. Nature.

> *A question about children of highly intellectual parents, how to work with them to transform things for them too.*

Parent work! We could talk for hours about how to love and understand the parents and help them to calm down. Everything you want to do with the children today, you have to do with the parents too. We have opened our foundation year at Sound Circle Center to parents, so that parents can come just for the sake of being in art again, singing and so on. It's a godsend. But it's too time-intensive for everybody.

And then, one must not moralize and make them feel even worse, because it's hard to be a parent. There are so many books out, all so contradictory. These poor parents swing from one extreme to another. I feel with them. They really, really want the best, and they do not know how to do that. Parent work is so important.

Now we have reached the end of our time together, and we have to stop with a feeling that is so much a part of childhood, the feeling not that it's all done and we're finished, but that there are so many things we still want to do. That's the limbs. The head would say, "I'm done." But the limbs say, "I want more!" So with that, I send you off.

Introduction
LECTURES BY DR. KARNOW

The question of "difficult children" is one that is echoing through our educational world today. These dear children are striving and struggling to find the path into healthy incarnation through the obstacles of modern life. Their struggles call upon us as educators to observe, understand, and respond to them with healing gestures.

We were privileged to have Dr. Gerald Karnow address these issues at the annual WECAN East Coast Conference in Spring Valley, New York, over three years from 2008-2010. Building from year to year, his lectures contain a rich content that considers both the child and the teacher. Dr. Karnow describes how the form of the child's physical body, growth rhythms, physical behavior, and awakening consciousness constantly communicate to us about his development. The educator needs to develop the observation skills and sensing organs to notice all the child is "speaking" to us. Another task is to learn to make our observation selfless by creating a sacred space within ourselves into which the child's being can speak without fear of being judged.

Dr. Karnow gives tools to help us understand the developmental steps with our thinking, to sense the child's states of soul and consciousness through our thinking-feeling, and to let these pictures stimulate our will to find the right healing response. Practicing these suggestions will help us develop flexibility, creativity, and compassion to meet the current and future, yet-unknown challenges the children will bring toward us. Printed together in this volume, the power of the lectures increases as they build from one to another. There is much here for repeated reading and contemplation.

—Nancy Blanning

Living and Working With So-Called Difficult Children PART I

SUMMARY BY NANCY BLANNING

The theme of this conference acknowledges that there are growing numbers of children who challenge us. Dr. Karnow asked what methods we employ to understand the "difficult child." What are our criteria for what is normal? If we provide age-appropriate content, then the children should, within a certain spectrum, be able to accommodate what the teacher brings. This assumes that we are bringing age-appropriate, Waldorf-inspired content, which permits the maturation of the child's individuality through the lower senses (touch, life, self-movement, and balance). This builds a physicality that will provide the framework for a healthy development of the higher senses (hearing, word, thought, and ego.) The careful working to build health in lower sense activity will provide the right foundation for later, more subtle, soul-spiritual development. The early childhood educator helps prepare the child in his body for grade school and the experience of the middle senses (smell, taste, sight, and warmth), and for the high school where the area of experience is the upper senses. The early childhood domain is the lower senses, the body, the will.

As we begin to consider "difficult" children, Dr. Karnow emphasized that it is essential to understand that all experiences we bring to the child through education affect physical development. This was illustrated by the example of Otto Specht, Rudolf Steiner's first student, which can serve as an archetype for our work as educators. Otto Specht was a hydrocephalic boy whose case was considered hopeless. To educate him was thought impossible. Nonetheless, the mother of this boy had trust in Rudolf Steiner and asked him to take on the boy's education. Steiner required that he alone would decide everything done with the boy, to which the mother agreed. He very closely structured the curriculum given to Otto and guided the movement of his limbs in very specific ways. Through these activities, the size of Otto's head shrank. He not only improved physically but completed his education and became a medical doctor. In this situation, Steiner was a young man educating a difficult child. This child could not learn and was essentially deformed. But through the education Steiner developed, the child not only improved his intellectual capacities and completed his education, but his physical body changed as well.

Each child wants to incarnate into the physical world and bring "the latest news from the spiritual world." The question for us is, does today's education create a body that the spiritual being of the child can inhabit? "Difficult" children are confronting a struggle in finding home in an earthly body.

Dr. Karnow described that in the first period of life, the child is all body, and all experiences affect body development. Everything we do affects the totality of the whole being, even through chemical and morphological changes that occur in the body. Not only the soul life — emotional, intellectual, and psychological — is affected. In other words, everything we do with the young child affects his physicality, his physical body. Pedagogical activities work upon the physical, while the medical activities work on the etheric. What we present in the pedagogy is received through the senses and works deeply into the body. Regarding the "difficult" child, the physical body can be the bridge through which we can foster healthy development through the educational experiences we bring.

The physical body can also be the vehicle through which we can come to understand the "difficult" child. The ability to observe is key in approaching perplexing children. Dr. Karnow remarked that when he goes to a school as physician, he does so with anxiety. He is asked to observe, and he follows Rudolf Steiner's guidelines as to what to do — just look. One has to empty oneself of anxiety, having trust that some insight will come. Something catches our attention toward that child, perhaps a heavy ear lobe that does not tell anything by itself. It has to connect to something else, a movement, perhaps. Dr. Karnow quoted from the first chapter of *Fundamentals of Therapy*: "It is of the utmost importance to know that the human being's ordinary forces of thinking are refined form and growth forces. A spiritual element reveals itself in the forming and growing of the human organism. And this spiritual element then appears during the course of later life as the spiritual power of thought." When we observe soul behavior, such as speech, movement, movement of thoughts, forgetting, and so on, we will only find the answer to why the behavior is occurring by looking back at the body itself.

This is where the physician is a helpful colleague to the educator. The teacher looks at the soul and describes the soul manifested in the child's behavior. The doctor lives in relation to the body. The doctor is asked to give a reason for why the child is unable to behave differently. Up to about age twenty-one, we see organically driven behavior and we want to understand what its cause. Early childhood teachers are dealing with organ-driven behavior, determined by the child's physicality.

There needs to be a dialogue between doctor and teacher. How can we understand behaviors that stir our interest, or that annoy? We understand behavior is organically driven. So what are we to do about it? Otto Specht's behavior was organically determined. His physical condition did not allow him to participate in a normal school. So Rudolf Steiner saw he had to evoke a change in the organism. If we want to evoke a change in behavior, we have to evoke a change in the organism. We usually come up with reasons derived from things in the child's environment to account for difficult behaviors—media, diet, family life—but the true answer lies in the physical body of the child.

Yet how can we come to truly observe the child so that we can gain a sense for what to do to evoke a beneficial change? Dr. Karnow spoke of times past when human beings had active converse with the gods in mystery centers, the sources of spiritually revealed knowledge in ancient times. Rudolf Steiner states in Volume Six of *Karmic Relationships* that whatever originates in medicine today is fundamentally an aftermath from insights shared by the ancient Mercury gods. But things have run dry in our times. Humanity must rediscover how to have new conversation with divine beings. To help us do that is the mission of anthroposophy.

If we think of our work as a process of entering the spiritual world and being guided by the beings who live in it, this gives meaning to our work that transcends the moment and deepens our task. Every Waldorf school is a mystery center, but only if we realize it and act accordingly. This we can do through the gifts given by Rudolf Steiner through anthroposophy.

In his *Difficult Children* book, Henning Köhler speaks of our coming into relationship with the "difficult" child as a path of initiation, a conscious entry into relation to the spiritual world. How can one undergo this initiation? One needs to create a posture of creative "not-knowing." We want to go into a situation not knowing anything and thereby create an organ of "not- knowing" receptivity. This needs intense participation. The observer enters into a situation where the being of the contemplated child actually melts into oneself; observer and the one observed become one.

This is an act of emptying out and becoming selfless, of not being burdened by ideas, preconceptions, or expectations, but of being open. The nose or ear or hands or feet or movement or tone of voice could capture our attention. To become one with another, the observer has to become empty, still, quiet, and warm. If one does that, the inspiration of what needs to happen will come. Steiner calls this a "thinking-feeling" into the other. Then the observer will be "thought" by the being of the child as act of creative identification. I become one with you. This is a turning around of the activity of an educator or observer from what is customary. It is a non-labeling approach. It is totally open, and one does not know what is going to happen. True communication, true dialogue can happen when this emptying has occurred.

To achieve this emptying requires enormous inner work on the part of the educator. Labeling a child as "difficult" points to something in ourselves rather than the child. We admit we cannot handle this child in the context of the other children. This child explodes the bubble in which we want our children to be contained. We want the children to do just what we want. Dr. Karnow referred to Köhler's observation that one of the biggest impediments to our moving forward is our addiction to contentment. In our classrooms, we want everything to be harmonious and nice. When we are led by this desire to be comfortable, we are not open to hearing the true child speak.

The point stands out from Köhler's book that we need a new artistic mode of educational thinking and observing. When we look at something artistically, the form we perceive becomes an expression of what created that form. Through the form, we can begin to see the invisible aspects of the human being. To do this, we have to learn to grow wings. The visible is a kind of darkness, an abyss. This is what we see when we just look at the outer physicality. We need to develop wings to penetrate through the darkness and see the spark of light and be able to bring it to birth, to save it.

Throughout the lectures, Dr. Karnow made repeated reference to his pedagogical "bibles" — *Study of Man* and *Curative Education*. These two are courses in "wing development." The answers to all our questions lie in these two books. He urged teachers to commit dedicated study to these volumes. We can grow wings by taking up spiritual ideas about the nature of the human being. To appreciate the threefold nature of humanity, which these lectures describe, gives us eyes to see with and wings to fly over the chasm that separates us from an understanding of the child. Especially when we meet together in a circle, sharing our different perspectives, we can perceive and become participants in creative forces that give us tools for understanding and tools for working.

Dr. Karnow reminded us that life is structured in time. Human development is a process in time. Our society is one that expects quick answers and solutions, so this process puts us at odds with modern expectations. As educators, we have to understand that what is done with a child now will have its results in the future, in later life. As helping companions to the child, we must also have patience that the dialogue with the true spiritual being of the child will not happen instantly. The processes of emptying, looking, listening, and sensing require time and patience. We must be able to withstand the discomfort we feel in not being able to come up with an answer right away. We have to wait to permit the world to imprint itself into us so we can realize the meaning of what we see. This requires patience and tolerance to live with the frustration of not having a quick answer.

In his opening remarks, Dr. Karnow shared a verse given by Rudolf Steiner to Dr. Ita Wegman, which pictures the theme through the three days of lectures:

> *The human being is a bridge*
> *Between the past and future existence.*
> *The present is a moment; moment as bridge.*
> *Spirit grown to soul in matter's husk*
> *Comes from the past.*
> *Soul growing to spirit as seed encased*
> *Journeys toward the future.*
> *Grasp future things through past ones*
> *Hope for evolving things through what has evolved.*
> *So grasp existence in evolving growth;*
> *So grasp what will be in what exists.*
> DEC. 21, 1921

This verse is spoken at the faculty meetings of the Otto Specht School, a new curative endeavor in the Fellowship Community. It was begun to offer another program to carry "difficult" children whom the regular classroom cannot embrace. The program's existence points squarely to questions we teachers carry: Is Waldorf education here for all children? Can this education meet every child's needs? Dr. Karnow answered this. Yes, we are here for all children, but there may be circumstances where we cannot meet all the children's needs. If a child is asked to leave, we must be honest and clear as to why. Is it because we are addicted to contentment, or because it is truly impossible? There are situations where a child is carried despite difficulties and where, through time, a transformation has occurred. We must keep in mind the time element.

We can also remind ourselves that Waldorf education is confined not only to a nice classroom. The world is a classroom, as it is a mystery temple. Waldorf education can happen everywhere, and some children require this wider vista. Every situation of daily life can become curriculum for Waldorf education. An attempt to realize this is being made at the Otto Specht School, which has the benefit of being situated in a community for the elderly. It is surrounded by woods and streams, large gardens, greenhouses, an orchard, and a dairy farm with sheep and chickens, all permitting creative educational efforts.

To conclude, Dr. Karnow returned to Henning Köhler's statement that difficult children do not exist. Children with difficult behaviors do. We need to develop a knowing-understanding through an "emptying-out" attitude, where we do not label, we do not react. The children need us to say "yes" to them, which will be our virtue development because they require us to be on a path of inner development. We can picture ourselves as musicians who "lift" our musicianship to a soul capacity where we can bring about social harmony and create music in social situations. The children who experience this lifting into selfless, social skills will be affected in their bodies. We affect the children's bodies by who we are and what we do. This fundamental transformation of attitude — saying "yes" to the child — is what is required.

The final keynote lecture ended with these words: Yes, Waldorf education is for every child. No, we cannot always meet the needs of every child. Yes, life is difficult. Life is beautiful.

Living and Working With So-Called Difficult Children PART II
SUMMARY BY NANCY BLANNING

Dr. Karnow's presentations began with the following verse, which Rudolf Steiner gave to Dr. Ita Wegman in December, 1921.

> *The human being is a bridge*
> *Between the past and future existence.*
> *The present is a moment; moment as bridge.*
> *Spirit grown to soul in matter's husk*
> *Comes from the past.*
> *Soul growing to spirit as seed encased*
> *Journeys toward the future.*
> *Grasp future things through past ones*
> *Hope for evolving things through what has evolved.*
> *So grasp existence in evolving growth;*
> *So grasp what will be in what exists.*

This image can serve as a bridge as well to contemplating the second major topic Dr. Karnow offered in his keynote addresses. The first theme considered what mood of soul the teacher must develop in order to understand and serve the child. We need to cultivate selfless emptiness so the being of the child can speak into us and guide us in what to do. We must shed our sympathies and antipathies, our expectations and judgments about the child. We let the development and experiences of the child resonate within us and then guide us into future action on the child's behalf. We do not label. We develop reality-based thoughts formed not on abstract ideas, but upon what we observe.

This leads to the second major theme, observation of the child as a threefold being. Dr. Karnow described that Rudolf Steiner worked for thirty years before he shared the content of his thoughts on the threefold organization of the human being. These are ideas we need to work with more and more seriously, as this threefold picture is the motif of our work. This gives an approach to understand the **time structure** of the human life so we can begin to know what to do. When we are working with the "difficult" child, we are struggling to understand the threefold nature of the human being.

This time structure and the threefold human being are discussed in *Riddles of the Soul*. Rudolf Steiner perceived through his years of research that the human being has three aspects which find expression in both the physical body and in soul activities. There is the nerve-sense system (including the brain and nerves), the rhythmic system (including the heart and lungs), and the metabolic-limb system. These are the physical expressions of this threefold nature. Connected to these systems are soul activities of thinking, feeling, and willing, respectively. The physical base for thinking is the nerve-sense system. Feeling, emotional life, lives not in the nerve-sense system but rather in the rhythmic system. In conventional psychology, everything is assumed to function within the nervous system, but Steiner's observation-based research said that this is not so. Feeling life lives in the rhythmic system. Willing activity lives in the metabolic-limb system. Steiner states in *Riddles of the Soul*:

> *Just as, when something is mentally pictured, a nerve process occurs upon which the soul becomes conscious of its mental picturing, and just as, when something is felt, a modification of the breathing rhythm takes place through which a feeling arises in the soul: so when something is willed, a metabolic process happens, which is the bodily foundation for what is experienced in the soul as willing.*

The *whole* physical/physiological human being is the basis of the life of soul, not just the nervous system. For those active in Waldorf education, to make the above observations may seem commonplace. We speak of thinking, feeling, and willing all the time. But Dr. Karnow emphasized it is important that we consider these deeply; these are vast ideas and profound insights. Truly understanding the development and expression of thinking, feeling, and willing can be the "foundation stone" for the teacher's work.

Rudolf Steiner further explains that thinking, feeling, and willing develop in the course of time. Aspects of these physical and soul processes, which operate in time, permeate the whole human being; yet each system is also identified with a physical region as well. The head, the physical center of the sensory and nervous systems, has its concentrated development during the first seven years of life. The trunk and rhythmic system have focused development, leading toward maturity, in years seven to fourteen. And development of the metabolism and limb system is the focal point between the ages of fourteen to twenty-one, when the body fills out and develops muscles and a solid physical form.

While this development, which we can physically see, is occurring, there is also development occurring for an "invisible" human during these seven-year periods. From birth to age seven, the etheric body—the body of formative forces—is growing and molding the physical body. From seven to fourteen, the astral body—the body of consciousness, of sympathy and antipathy—is educating the feeling life. Then from fourteen to twenty-one, the I or ego force is working to grow and strengthen independent thinking forces which can flow into deed through the human will.

When each of these "invisible" bodies has completed its work in these ways, it is liberated for new tasks in the soul life. These soul elements of thinking, feeling, and willing are not only rooted in the physical body but undergo liberation and transformation when bodily processes complete their phases of development. The energies which have been dedicated to physical growth become available for new processes in the soul life. Specifically, the first seven-year period completes the forming of the child's physical body through the activity of etheric growth forces. Then the forming activity is transformed into powers of thought.

This is described in the first chapter of *Fundamentals of Therapy* by Rudolf Steiner and Ita Wegman:

> *Forces functioning in the ether body are active at the beginning of the human being's life on earth—most distinctly during the embryonal period—as the forces of formation and growth. During the course of earthly life a portion of these forces emancipates itself from this occupation with formation and growth and becomes forces of thinking, just those forces which, for the ordinary consciousness bring forth the shadowlike world of thoughts.*

> *It is of the utmost importance to know that the human being's ordinary forces of thinking are refined form and growth forces. A spiritual element reveals itself in the forming and growing of the human organism. And this spiritual element then appears during the course of later life as the spiritual power of thought.*

That which forms the body comes to a level of completion and is now available to be forces that allow us to have content in our mind. We have a visible human being forming—the physical body which we can experience with our physical senses. As this attains completion in its formation, the "invisible" human being is being born. The true bridge spanning the past into the future manifests only when the invisible I or individuality is born. Before the birth of the I, everything is from the past. Our capacity to think comes from the transformed forces that have formed and grown the physical body. How we think is grounded in what type of form we have accomplished in the physical body. If we can observe and understand the *form* of the body, then we can develop windows into understanding how thinking, feeling, and willing manifest themselves. The physical human being has a physical physiology; the invisible human-coming-into-being also has a soul-spiritual physiology. As we observe children's behavior, we are actually talking about an anatomy of the soul. This anatomy of soul is rooted in the physical body, in the substance of the human body.

Now Steiner takes this picture of the threefold human being yet a further step. He points out that each of the seven-year periods has within itself a threefold aspect as well. He states in *Soul Economy*: "One can recognize such seven-year periods throughout the entire course of human life, and each of these periods again falls into three clearly differentiated shorter periods." The big seven-year phases mentioned above follow the developmental motifs of nerve/sense system, rhythmic system, and metabolic/limb system respectively. Yet within each seven-year period, there is a mini-recapitulation of these developmental motifs.

Since our work as early childhood educators is primarily concerned with the time from birth to age seven, we will use that as the focus for our consideration here. From birth to two years and four months, development concentrates upon the nerve/sense system and is most visible in the development of the head. From that point until four years and eight months of age, the rhythmic system is in the forefront, and changes in trunk are the visible physical expressions of development. In the final stage, which lasts through the seventh year, the maturation achieved in the metabolic/limb system shows itself through structural changes in the arms and legs.

From this physical picture, let us return to consideration of what is happening with the "invisible" soul development for the child. When this growth task is completed, the etheric forces become available for use by soul activities. In *Soul Economy*, Steiner states: "Now, at the end of the first seven-year period, most of these etheric forces are released to flow into the child's soul and spiritual nature." He points out that

> *a supersensible contemplation of man will reveal to us, apart from his physical body, another finer body which we have called the etheric body or the body of formative forces. From this etheric body spring not only all the forces sustaining nourishment and growth, but it is also the source of the faculties of remembering and of making mental images, of ideation. It becomes an independent entity only during the change of teeth, at which time it is born in a similar way in which, at physical birth, the body is born from its mother. This means that up to the change of teeth the forces of the etheric body are entirely working in the processes of the child's organic growth, whereas after that time—though still remaining active in this realm to a great extent—they partly withdraw from these activities. These released forces of the ether body now begin to work in the soul realm of mental picturing and memory, as well as in the many other nuances of the child's soul life.*

When the etheric forces have achieved a certain completion in growth of the physical body, those forces are liberated for the soul activities of thinking, feeling, and willing. With each visible, physical completion come changes in the behavior and consciousness of the child. This is true for each full seven-year cycle as a whole and also for the threefold divisions of each larger cycle. As the etheric body completes its growth tasks, this body of formative energies becomes available for soul activity in thirds as well. So we will see changes in consciousness, emotional and will life in distinct thirds within each seven-year period, too.

The more we study human development, the more we will be able to observe the changes in consciousness that correspond with physical developmental completions. The changes in physical form will guide us into knowing whether different soul capacities have been liberated for the tasks of school, for example. If the physical development is incomplete or atypical, as will often be true with the "difficult" child, we can begin to understand why and how there may also be unusual aspects of behavior and consciousness, which are the expressions of the "invisible" human soul. By looking at outward forms of the human body, we practice a special kind of perceiving. Dr. Karnow described this as a flexible "seeing thinking," a kind of conscious clairvoyance where the thinking is willed into us by the child.

Dr. Karnow emphasized Steiner's insight that points of physical development and changes in conscious soul life are not only related but are interdependent. If we truly school ourselves to know what these changes are, we will have a map guiding us in our child observation. We must know what is normal and typical for the child and appropriate to each age phase before we can begin to observe deviations or exceptions which the difficult child might present. Knowing the hallmarks of these nodal points is essential in helping us observe whether developmental completion has been achieved and a child is ready to go on to a next step, such as going on to first grade.

A primary source for understanding the threefold division of the seven-year phases is Dr. Bernard Lievegoed's *Phases of Childhood*. Dr. Karnow has added this volume to the pedagogical "bibles" of *Study of Man* and *Education for Special Needs*. Dr. Lievegoed took the indications so briefly sketched above and gave detailed descriptions of how these developments are manifested in both the physical body and in the soul life in thinking, feeling, and willing. It is not possible in this article to do justice to the detailed and precise descriptions he offers to guide the teacher's observation of the child. The book is a masterwork that deserves dedicated study. Below are offered only some of the basic motifs to help us develop a framework for organizing our own picturing of these processes.

Dr. Lievegoed begins by pointing out how the proportion of head size to the rest of the body changes. In a baby the proportion of head to body is 1:4. Up to about two years, the head predominates as the focal point, due to its size. By two years, the ratio has changed to 1:5, and by age six to 1:6. Until a new growth spurt begins at about age two, with growth in the trunk area, the upper half of the baby's body predominates. "The upper half of the body runs ahead of the lower half; the head in relation to the trunk, the shoulders in relation to the pelvis, the skull in relation to the facial structure, the eye sockets in relation to the lower jaw, and so on."

From about two-and-a-half to five years, the toddler figure is evident. With the head-to-body proportion now reduced to a 1:5 ratio, growth is seen in the trunk. At this time growth in height occurs mostly through stretching in the trunk region, not in the limbs. There is primarily growth in breadth of the body, with a characteristic large tummy, and the angle at the bottom of the rib cage still flat. On the head, the chin has come more forward and gives the face more expression.

From five to seven years, there is dramatic growth in the limbs, as they grow longer and more slender. A waist develops, the stomach grows flat, the spine develops an S-shaped curve, and the collarbones become more pronounced. Body movements appear more angular and more purposeful.

The body develops greater freedom of movement and there is much motor activity of the whole body.

The school-ready child will show physical aspects, as the face begins to change around the age of seven, marking the beginning of a whole new phase. By this time the head to body ratio is 1:6. The eyes, which have been below the halfway line of the head until now, have moved upward, making the forehead less dominant. The eyes now appear smaller in the face and can look expectant and more conscious, observing the world with some judgment. Dr. Lievegoed describes that "the whole impression is one of slim agility and easy, comfortable mobility, of an elegance which was lacking in the toddler." Children tend to be rather thin at this stage, as well.

There is parallel development of soul life of the little child as well. Up through the first two years at least, the child is an open sense organ who responds through the body to all things that come into her sensory life. Experiences and expressions of pleasure or pain, joy or sadness are body-based. Emotions depend on the state of the physical organism. Behavior is based on drives of the body.

The toddler, in roughly the second third of the first seven-year period, begins to become aware of the world as something separate from her. She is not only influenced by the world but begins to influence it as well. Play arises in an exchange with the environment. The imagination for play arises out of what is in the child's surroundings, not out of an inner imagination which marks the next step of development. The child can respond to the world only in the present moment. She plays with things in her horizon, with what is available *now*. Play can take on a rhythmic quality that seems to flow in an imaginative stream. Behavior is no longer based primarily upon drives. The child at this age loves to live in rhythms which can smoothly carry her along.

With the beginning of the final third, a big change comes in play and imaginative life. The child is able to take a step back from the world and consider it, rather than be so directed by it. Lievegoed calls this "creative imagination," which stands separate from the world and which can imaginatively change the environment as play dictates. The environment is used to create the inwardly-held play imagination rather than suggest or even dictate to the child what to play. Play has a goal directed by the child's will. In practical life, the child begins to be aware of what he can do and be frustrated by what he cannot achieve according to his own expectations. He begins to look to the adults in his environment and to respect them for what they *can do* rather than by what they intellectually *know* or attempt to explain to him.

Dr. Lievegoed summarizes: during the period from birth to seven, the first third is dedicated to developing the foundation of the nerve/sense system of head, senses, and nerves as the foundation for later thinking. At its conclusion, the etheric force births itself from the head region. The second third shows development in the young child's feeling life and the emergence of creative imagination. The etheric forces liberate from the trunk region at this phase's end. The final third shows development of intentional will, as the child forms an inner imagination which he then executes in the world through his will. The final partial birthing of the etheric forces is achieved when the limbs show the mature and elongated form of the school-ready child.

A general summary relating to each of the seven-year phases from birth to twenty-one is further given by Dr. Lievegoed:

> *Every metamorphosis in thinking coincides with an important change in the appearance of the head, the expression of the face.*
>
> *The periods of the changes in feeling correspond to the periods of growth in breadth of the trunk.*
>
> *The critical periods in the development of the will coincide with moments of growth in height, when the limbs in particular grow much longer.*

As shown above, this is certainly true for the first seven years. It also applies to the changes in physical growth and of consciousness seen during the cycles of the school-aged child and of the adolescent.

This consideration began with the image of a "bridge" which connects the past with the future. Dr. Karnow stated that the true bridging occurs with the birth of the I, the true individuality of the human being. What have been described above are all steps along the way to the resounding birth of the I at age twenty-one. How well that event will occur depends mightily upon how each of these earlier steps and developmental phases were completed.

As teachers, we are "incarnational" guardians for the children. What we provide for them in early childhood is important for the whole of life, not just for this immediate time during which they are in our care. We serve the children well when we know what archetypal developmental stages are, both physically and in terms of consciousness, in emotional life, and in the expression of the child's will. Only then can we observe when development is proceeding in a healthy fashion and when there are impediments to the incarnation process. If we know the hallmarks of development, we can observe where things are on an archetypal course and where there may be delays or incongruities. If we can observe the match or mismatch of chronological age and developmental manifestation, we can gain a sense of where the child may be frustrated or stuck in development and gain sympathy for his or her struggles. This opening up to the child's situation can inspire insight into the "difficult" child and guide us to help the child move beyond the obstacle in his or her path.

This series began with considering the inner work of the teacher. This educational guardian must strive to develop a selfless emptiness, which becomes an open space into which the being of the child can speak. This second article has attempted to expand our understanding of what is a true picture of the human being in early childhood. This concluding thought from *Soul Economy* by Rudolf Steiner ties these threads together:

> *What really matters in education is the mood and attitude of soul, which the teacher carries in his heart with regard to the being of man . . . What really matters is that each teacher carries within himself a true picture of man and if this picture stands there before his inner gaze, he or she will act rightly, though outwardly possibly in very different ways.*

Developing the Eyes to See
SUMMARY BY NANCY BLANNING

The early childhood educator is sometimes a "magician," a "priestess" or "priest" who sings form into being. This was the opening picture Dr. Gerald Karnow shared with the early childhood educators at the February 2009 East Coast Early Childhood Conference, *Developing the Eyes to See*. He described how he had observed kindergarten classes where he saw apparent chaos while the children played. Yet the chaos was highly structured. Within it he could perceive developing organs of interacting groups, mobile flow forms, messes, battles, and intimate relationships developing. When the chaos lost its organization for a moment, the teacher sang a song. The children suddenly moved into a circle and heard a story from which they moved to put the room into perfect order. The children knew just what to do. When he sees this in an early childhood class, it is utter, beautiful magic.

These experiences reminded Dr. Karnow of an image from Rudolf Steiner's lectures, *Cosmic Memory*. A priestess sings to a group of people. They move in relationship to what she sings, and the song deeply impresses itself into those who listen. Something is structured through the song into these human beings. Recalling the thoughts presented from the previous year, Dr. Karnow re-emphasized that everything the children experience in our classes literally forms their physical being—as well as their social and psychical being—for the rest of life. Our intention and responsibility as educators is to connect what the children have brought from the past with lawful activities to form and guide their future. To do this rightly, we must find ways through our inner development to become priestly.

The guidance to achieve this comes to us through spiritual science, anthroposophy. In the "teaching bibles," *Study of Man* (or *The Foundations of Human Experience*) and *Curative Education* (*Education for Special Needs*), Rudolf Steiner gives a reality-based understanding of the human being that embraces our spiritual nature as well as the sense-perceptible form. Deeply studying these works gives us common ground for building Waldorf education communities. Through time, humanity has become more distant from the divine worlds. Anthroposophy offers us means to re-establish that connection and to work for redemption of the human being from the materialistic picture that dominates today. This requires conscious study and disciplined will to grasp these ideas and bring them into actual practice. This can give us enormous enthusiasm in perceiving the priestly task of the early childhood educator. Yet, cautioned Dr. Karnow, enthusiasm must be filled with real content. Without content, things become sentimental. The children do not need sentimental educators but ones grounded in spiritual-scientific knowledge.

Our understanding has to be grounded in realizing that the little child is entirely a sense organ standing in a devotional mood to what surrounds him. All experiences are taken in, "eaten," indiscriminately. What the child takes in is consumed and works to structure the body. Not just the physical environment is consumed but also the movement, speech, and inner life of the teacher. Our attitudes and moods, as well as actions, change the child's breathing, circulation, and metabolic functions, the child's whole physiology. We wish to be mediators and creative priests who surround the children with a world worthy of imitation supporting healthy development. Consequently, we must observe what is happening within our own souls.

We must also develop eyes to truly *see* the children. Seeing involves more than the common idea that the human eye is like a camera that creates a visual image. Seeing also involves moving and touching with invisible hands and arms that reach out and touch the world through our gaze. This permits us to identify with and become one with what we are seeing. The children we direct our interest and attention toward want to be perceived and acknowledged as the true spiritual beings they are. In our seeing, we open and empty ourselves to experience the child as though we were that other human being. This is the kind of communication we strive for. Through our knowledge of child development, we have to provide an environment that draws the children into this relationship with us.

Dr. Karnow now returned to expanding and refining the picture of the young child up to the change of teeth. Rudolf Steiner emphasized repeatedly that etheric forces in the child are dedicated to physical growth rather than thinking consciousness up to the change of teeth. The same etheric forces, through which the child grows, are liberated at the change of teeth to be available for thinking. (See Steiner and Wegman, *Fundamentals of Therapy*, Chapter One.) The ability to intentionally direct attention and consciousness is not at the child's disposal before this point. Rather, the body grows and changes and consciousness emerges in three stages from birth to about age seven (see Lievegoed and Schoorel for further description of these phases). Consciousness and attention are still body-bound in young children, as is their behavior. We must have an accurate picture of how development unfolds in order to observe what is typical, healthy development in a child and what is not.

Rudolf Steiner divided human development into seven-year periods—birth to seven years, seven to fourteen years, fourteen to twenty-one—and then each of these periods is subdivided into three parts. Each state results in the development and birthing of a particular aspect of the human being. The time we are essentially concerned with is birth to seven and its three divisions. Within these one-third divisions, certain aspects will lawfully arise if the child is developing in a healthy way. If we know the nature of each of these segments, we will know what is appropriate to ask of the child at each stage. If we demand activities too early, we can cause etheric damage.

We can see how the child is being affected by the environment through watching how the child responds to what we do. If we see that certain organic, physiological events have not happened, we cannot demand that the child perform intellectual activities without damaging the child's physical body. This is the kind of *seeing* that we are striving to develop within ourselves.

Development in the first seven years proceeds from the head downward through the nerve-sense system. In these years we see growth and changes in the physical body accompanied by changes and development in the child's consciousness. The child "communicates" its development to us through changes in body and behavior rather than in words or intentionally directed deeds. In understanding the right kind of communication at these stages, we can come to judgment of how development is progressing.

Dr. Karnow went on to characterize the changes in consciousness and awareness that correspond with these one-third segments. A baby in arms, for example, is caught in the human warmth relationship with the mother, not with external objects or people. From birth until this time, the child is intimately bound to the organization of the mother and needs to be nourished in her own etheric formation through this connection. Everything of the body is round and "head." As consciousness gradually emerges during the first seven years, it shows itself as a purely reflective or mirroring consciousness. At about two years and four months, the etheric formative forces are freed from the head. Physically the head features are becoming more defined and pronounced. In behavior, this change is also marked by the child completely mirroring its environment through imitation. This stage marks the beginning of cognitive intelligence.

The middle period from two and four months through about four years and eight months begins relationship formation. Forces are freed that permit relationship to develop with others besides just the mother. Social development begins. This is the sphere of feeling life, demonstrated physically through the development of the rhythmic system. The head form now recedes and we see a change in the trunk through separation of the belly from the chest. Imitation here is based on relationship, and social and emotional intelligence begins development during this phase.

In the last stage the limbs lengthen. Willing aspects of the body are freed from the metabolic-limb system and are available for doing things. The child physically becomes long and dangly. The child moves from the rounded aspect of the first third to a more linear form. Play becomes much more goal directed. Objects do not matter so much for what they are themselves but for what they can be made into. This can be called limb and skills intelligence.

Children will go to what they need within their environment. It is our responsibility to provide the right environment, which allows and supports these developmental stages to be explored. Observing where and how the children interact with the environment and play helps us read the developmental stage of the child.

Uniting these observations with the other things we notice brings us to child study. In child study, we never want to judge. We do child study only to deepen our insight into knowing what to do that is helpful for the child. Treatment, for the doctor, comes out of understanding the problem; inherent in the diagnosis lies the remedy and treatment. This is true for the educator as well. We strive to understand the dynamics of the child—physical development and outer form, outer movement, inner soul movement, social behavior, and so on—so we can understand and help.

One dynamic we can use in our observation for child study is between round and linear. The nerve-sense system is linear and deadened. Through the nature of the nerves, we are able to have consciousness. Children with very awake consciousness are often thin and pale, and vice versa. The nerve-sense system predominates and intellectual precocity will probably be seen. Dr. Karnow described a child of this nature who was quiet and observing, not interacting. She was having difficulty placing herself into relationship with the world. In its furthest extreme, this inclination leans toward autism.

On the opposite side is the metabolic-limb system, the blood pole. A child Dr. Karnow described here was one who was short, compact, and ruddy, and also very active and prone to bumping. Everything was a little overdone in a "hysterical" reaching out to others. Here there is excessive working of the blood so behavior is uncontained.

In both of these cases, if the inclinations described proceed into the future, we can anticipate problems for the child. How can we bring nerve activity to cool the blood? We bring conceptual activity and love. How do we bring life to a dead nerve? We bring blood activity to balance the excessive nerve dominance through enthusiasm and love. The particulars of how to do this are ours to discern. Our profound interest in the child will lead to the details of what to do with these two gestures of cooling and warming. When we remind ourselves that everything we do as educators affects the physiology of the child, we can know that what we offer can truly provide healing to such out-of-balance inclinations.

The blood and nerve poles are brought into connection through our breathing and feeling life. To learn how to activate the breathing needs to be part of our training. Educators become soul artists in learning how to appropriately speed up or slow down the child's breathing. Through doing this, Rudolf Steiner was literally able to change the physical body of his student, Otto Specht.

At the beginning of his talks, Dr. Karnow gave the picture of the kindergarten class during free play. When the children engaged in "chaotic" play and then found the way to order—in this case through the priestly singing—their breathing changed. At first the room felt like "a stable" and then it felt like "a church." Increasing breathing emphasizes the blood pole and slowing it down leads to wakefulness and consciousness, the nerve pole. We are in control of this and can use this insight to the children's benefit.

Dr. Karnow concluded by saying that we need to carry in ourselves the following statement from *Fundamentals of Therapy* in our blood and our hearts:

> *These forces functioning in the ether body are active at the beginning of the human being's life on earth—most distinctly during the embryonic period—as the forces of formation and growth. During the course of earthly life a portion of these forces emancipates itself from this occupation with formation and growth and becomes forces of thinking, just those forces which, for the ordinary consciousness bring forth the shadowlike world of thoughts.*

It is of the utmost importance to know that the human being's ordinary forces of thinking are refined form and growth forces. A spiritual element reveals itself in the forming and growing of the human organization. And this spiritual element then appears during the course of later life as the spiritual power of thought.

This power of thought is only one part of the human capacity for form and growth that weaves in the etheric. The other part remains true to the purpose it fulfilled in the beginning of the human being's life. Only because the human being continues to evolve even when his form and his growth are advanced, that is, when they are to a certain degree completed, does the etheric spiritual force, which lives and works in the organism, appear in later life as the power of thought (see Steiner and Wegman, Chapter One).

What we see in children's behavior arises out of the form of the body. To understand behavior, we have to look at the body, not with outer eyes, but stopping midway to read its form. We learn to know that there is meaning in every form. Our attentive observation will lead to understanding the dynamics at play within the child. The soul and spirit create the body and then emerge out of it step-by-step. The life forces, which formed the body, offer themselves first. Only when these forces do emerge, allowing consciousness, can we do thinking activities with the child.

Dr. Karnow urged us to work together and share our observations. Then we will develop "seeing" reality with multiple dimensions. There is the child's outer form with physical dimensions. There is also the inner form with soul dimensions, as well as the psychological dimensions of thinking, feeling, and willing. It is necessary to also perceive the spiritual dimension. How is the child striving to incarnate? To learn this, we must truly *see* the child in these multi-dimensional ways to dialogue with his or her being.

Deepening Our Capacities to Meet the Children in Our Care
SUMMARY BY NANCY BLANNING

Secretly, began Dr. Karnow, we should consider early childhood as the most important work in Waldorf education. The experiences in early childhood provide the foundation for all of life and are most crucial in facilitating healthy incarnation of the human being. Last year the work in our kindergartens was characterized as "priestly." A picture from Steiner's Cosmic Memory describes a grove where the priestess sings her listeners into becoming the vehicle for the incarnated spiritual "I." Her priestly deed was preparation for the human being to be able to say "I." Likewise, the task of Waldorf early childhood education is incarnation of the "I" in the children.

Another component of this secret is that it requires the greatest amount of selflessness on the part of the educator. What matters is not so much what we know as what we create around the children so the "I" can find the proper residence in the physical organism. We are the midwives, the priests, and potentially also the physicians for the children we work with—and for the parents and ourselves as well. This selflessness has to do with creating an environment that permits the "I" to experience itself. A powerful example of how the child comes to experience himself comes in Steiner's lecture, "Self-Education in the Light of Spiritual Science" (Berlin, March 14, 1912). Spiritual science appreciates that there is a higher Self acting upon the child outside of his normal self:

> *Besides what we take hold of as educators developing out of our*

normal consciousness, something is already working on the child as a higher being outside of his normal self. If we focus on this, we will perhaps find another kind of education at work on the child, whereas in our normal education we turn only to the personal self of the child.

Where do we find what works on the child as a higher Self, and which belongs to the child, but doesn't enter his consciousness? Astonishing but true: it is children's play, *the meaningful, well-carried-out play of all children that the higher Self works on. With the child's play we can only create preconditions for an education. What is accomplished in play happens basically through the self-activity of the child, through everything that cannot be confined to strict rules. Indeed, the essential, educational aspect of play is based on the fact that we call a halt to our rules and to all our arts of education and leave the child to his own impulses.*

For what does the child do when we leave him to his own impulses? When playing with external objects the child can try out whether this or that will work through his own activity. He brings his own will into activity, into movement. Because of the way in which the external objects behave under the influence of the will, it then happens that the child educates himself for life, simply through play, in a completely different way than through the influence of an older person or of someone's pedagogical principles. For this reason it is so very important that we mix as little of the rational or intellectual as possible into children's play. The more that play has to do with what cannot be comprehended but is simply beheld in its living character, the better it is.

We have to set ourselves aside to permit the real being of the child to enter; this can only happen during the first seven years. We selflessly remove ourselves to create an environment in which we can perceive the true being of the child through his play.

What is this environment in which the child can "self-educate"? The classroom during free play can seem a chaotic mess, yet it is a "mess" in which there lives order. There are little clusters of activity here and there. It is an incredible cauldron of chaotic but organized activity. At a secret sign, the classroom is miraculously brought back into form through an orderly activity. The differentiated chaos is brought into a social unity. In witnessing this himself, Dr. Karnow realized that the whole organism of the class—a new creation—is being entered into by the children; the past which the children bring with them is entering the present. The teacher provides the right circumstances that permit this entry to happen into a highly differentiated way. This entry happens through the portals of the foundational senses of touch, life, self-movement, and balance, which the children need to experience in both the indoor and outdoor classroom. The consciousness of the teacher in holding each child in mind and her conscientiousness in guiding all that happens during the day creates a "kindergarten bubble," a protective sheath that surrounds the group.

As the child is "self-educating," he is also being formed through the experiences that come to him through the environment. In the first seven years the child is literally forming as well as growing the physical body. What we are doing in Waldorf early childhood education is so transformative that it changes the physical body. That is part of the secret of our work. All the child experiences through the senses and the more subtle aspects of mood, warmth of soul, joyfulness, and rhythmic order influence how the child's body develops toward a healthy incarnation. As we understand this, we can appreciate how we can bring healing influences toward the children in our care. Rudolf Steiner learned this through work with his first student, Otto Specht, a boy with hydrocephalus who was thought to be ineducable. Through Rudolf Steiner's pedagogical methods, the size and form of the boy's head shrunk and he eventually became a medical doctor.

This series of conferences began two years ago with considering "difficult children" (based on the title of Henning Köhler's book, *Difficult Children: There Is No Such Thing*.) Otto Specht was Rudolf Steiner's "difficult child" through whom he developed the basis for what became Waldorf education twenty years later. Now nearing a century since the founding of the first Waldorf school, we encounter increasing numbers of children who fall into this "difficult" category. These are children whose incarnation is not going right; they struggle to find a comfortable and harmonious inhabitation of the physical body with their "I." That the child is having some incarnational problem is seen quickly through our irritability or annoyance because a child is not doing what he is supposed to. We lose patience and want to know what to do.

One step toward knowing what to do is to look to the child's bodily form as a way to understand the behaviors that perplex and challenge us. Consider that we have two children in a class displaying opposite tendencies. One is fearful and retreats into a corner. Another one annoyingly jumps right into everyone's face. We worry about both, wanting to encourage the first and contain the other so that we can create a whole, harmonious organism.

As a physician, Dr. Karnow sits and watches and notes the polarities of the two different children. He works from the idea that every behavior has its roots in the morphology, the form and structure, of the body. So he looks at forms, specifically the form of the face. On the quiet child he sees that the facial features are a bit flattened, as though held back. The child running around has a face that comes forward, enters into space. He looks at the forms and the child's movement or lack thereof—chaotic movement, headless movement. He begins to find a connection between outer behavior and the child's physical form. He comes to a preliminary conclusion that the quiet individuality is holding back from really being incarnated, is not pressing his features out into the world.

The other gesture of form is "I will stick myself into your business all the time and will not stop." This is an organic behavior that places itself into the classroom. This knowledge comes out of an inner participation in the form of the child, which can tell us a secret of how that individuality is entering into the body. This insight comes not out of judgment or criticism but of out of a deeply warmed interest in wanting to understand the child's formative gesture.

All of our observations, to be humanely objective and morally upright, must be founded on what Dr. Karnow calls "the rock." This "rock" is the image of humanity as a threefold being shared with us through Rudolf Steiner's insights. This is the image of mankind as a spiritual being. Through this image we hold and behold the child in reverence, not judgment. We can discover huge secrets about what an individuality brings into this life if we stand upon "the rock."

In our observation first we look, then we see, and finally we behold. These are all different activities, focusing our attention more and more intently. In the wonder of beholding, we become what we behold. Through our eyes we enter into what we are looking at. We experience what we behold as if we were that ourselves. We become "one with" through this process. We often "look" and do not "see." But when we "behold," we become "one with." This is the mood that must permeate our looking at a child so intimately. We must stand upon "the rock" to make discriminations in our beholding.

If we look at children's heads, we see how highly individual they are. The head is differentiated into regions that reflect thinking (forehead region), feeling (central part of face), and willing (the jaw area.) If, for example, we looked at the upper lips of children in the class, a short upper lip might suggest that maturation stopped and kept the lip up. Another one keeps the lip down all the time; what impression does that convey? A lower jaw thrust forward looks as if it will attack. If the behaviors fit these impressions, we can see that an aspect expressed in the form of the body has emancipated and expressed itself psychologically in behavior.

We can use this approach to observation in contemplating the form of the child—not only the face but also the whole head, ear, threefoldness of head-trunk-limbs, and so on. Then we see what imagination these suggest. What comes of imagination, coupled with objective but warmed consideration of the behaviors emancipated from the body form, can lead us to the inspiration and intuition of what to do for the child. What can we emphasize within or bring into the kindergarten environment that will have a balancing and harmonizing effect? How can we bring healing in the pedagogical realm?

A big question confronting us is when it is appropriate to bring in other therapies. Dr. Karnow's answer—when the child cannot be contained in the "kindergarten bubble." If the child's capacity to imitate does not fall within what we provide for the class, the child steps outside of our pedagogical domain and cannot relate in an ordered way to the breathing "chaos." Then we have to come to an understanding, a diagnosis (which literally means "understanding through and through") and see where we can bring something to achieve balance. We can seek the support of anthroposophic medicine and therapeutic eurythmy. In some cases, sensory integration/sensory processing therapies are allies where the child's issues lie beyond what can be sufficiently addressed through our classroom environments.

Throughout this lecture series, we have considered the first seven years as the time the child grows the healthy physical body through the support of the etheric body. Everything of the physical body has to be imbued with the etheric. The body creates its form and grows. When certain stages of growth are completed, the etheric body is emancipated from that task and becomes available for other activities. Previous lectures have described this process and how the forces of the etheric body are birthed in three stages, ultimately to be available for use as thinking forces. We can have a glimmer of this invisible etheric world when we look at a colored disk and then see the complementary color magically appear as a glow when we then gaze upon a white surface. Something of this freed etheric force we project outward, allowing us to participate in an invisible world.

The etheric body is hard to speak about because, though we live within it all the time, we are unaware of its presence, "asleep" to it. But we can wake up to this reality. Through our thinking forces, we actually take hold of these emancipated forces that rise out of our body. When we realize that we can consciously relate to what the etheric is, we have tools that we can and do work with, whether we know it or not.

We must know as educators that what we do with our emancipated ether body affects the world around us and every other human being we meet. For example, we can send our gaze to another—an etheric encounter—and that person experiences it. Through our work with the child in the first seven years, we are working to assist the proper emancipation of the child's etheric through the environment and our actual being. As we create the space and present ourselves, we work deeply into the being of the child. We can do that more consciously and effectively when we understand the subtle distinctions of the etheric body—the four ethers themselves.

We know that the physical body is highly differentiated. It has aspects relating to the four elements—mineral, water/fluid, air, and fire/warmth. The etheric body is also differentiated into four aspects that relate to the elements. The solid, mineral substance of the physical body has to be drawn into a living state. If a mineral part of the human being is not lifted up, it literally becomes solid, like a kidney stone. The aspect of the etheric body that lifts the solid into life is the life ether.

This is also true for fluids. Water also has to be kept alive and maintained in a living state. We know the truth of this when we see its failure in an older person with heavy, swollen legs. The ether which brings the fluid into life is known as the chemical/sound/tone ether. It is the light ether which works in the air, which we can read about in *Cosmic Memory* or *Occult Science*. Air and light ether work as opposites. Air fills in the space between things; light separates and creates borders, reveals distinctions. We experience warmth ether when we take outer warmth and make it inner warmth. Through the interaction of these ethers with earthly elements, we have forces that bring our bodily substance into a living state. We can positively support the living state of the child and his incarnation into earthly life when we intentionally work with the ethers in our classrooms.

Where are the ethers in the classroom? We can first consider warmth in both the physical and soul warmth we have in our classrooms. Warmth in whatever form influences all the children. Each child has her own warmth organization but is also affected by outer warmth in the room. We must make sure the children are warmly dressed. Whenever we consider these issues of warmth, we are working with the warmth ether.

How do we work with the air? We need to tend the physical air itself and then go to the light ether. We think we see light, but rather we experience the effects of the light ether's activity, which reveals things and brings about separation. The air has to be circulating and light ether present in the lighting of the room. It must not be too light or too dark.

Is there fluidity in the room? Rhythm, the interdependence of everything we have in the classroom, how we can go from one play area to another so the children can move with social harmony—these are all expressions of the chemical or tone ether. Yet it is not just harmony of objects and implements in the room, but harmony of the being of the teacher and the harmony between teachers that also matters.

And what is the life ether? It is joy. The life ether is that which always permits the creation of life. It is unending and always present.

All of these are practical things we can consider. How we work with these etheric subtleties in our thinking also offers the children something to grow upon. How can we get to know the ethers from the inside out? Of the warmth ether we ask, "What permeates everything?" It is the warmth ether that can penetrate everything. So when we enter a class, we send the warmth of our thought into everything, filling the space. Warmth has no barriers, but lifts and permeates all.

In order to get inside the light ether, one can ask, "What is revelation, what is unveiling?" Here we can experience our thoughts as making discriminations in our environment. We can see what is out of order in the environment, in relationships.

The chemical ether poses a question of what is harmonization, order, interdependence, transformation of one thing into another. How is that living within the room, within the children, within oneself?

And of the life ether, we ask, what is self-creating life?

The theme throughout the three-years' presentation of lectures has been how we can bring healing and wholeness to the children on their path into incarnation. The challenges thrust upon the children seem to grow only more complex and subtle. They sometimes seem even phantom-like, living in shadows that our light of ordinary thinking cannot reveal. To meet these darkened forces, the children need champions. Dr. Karl König, founder of the curative education Camphill movement, expressed this in a verse that Dr. Karnow shared.

> *There is a knighthood of our time*
> *Whose members do not ride through the darkness*
> *Of physical forests as of old,*
> *But through the forests of darkened minds.*
> *They are armed with a spiritual armor*
> *An inner sun makes them radiant.*
> *Out of them shines healing—*
> *Healing that flows from the knowledge of the*
> *Image of Mankind as a spiritual being.*
> *They must create inner order, inner justice,*
> *Peace and conviction in the darkness of our time.*

We have to form a knighthood where we can all shine our inner sun, no matter what is happening outside. Whatever we do in relation to the ethers will work deeply into the bodies of the children in our care. With these we are taking in the forces of the sun and permitting something to grow and thrive that will not otherwise work. Then we will be what Dr. König calls the knights who have "an inner sun."

Dr. Karnow reminded us of our indebtedness to Rudolf Steiner. From him we have the "image of Mankind as a spiritual being." There is nothing we do in Waldorf education that is not founded upon the insights of anthroposophy Rudolf Steiner so generously offers to us. We must never cease deepening our relationship with these fundamental sources. These insights are the "rock" upon which this new knighthood stands.

Bibliography

Dr. Steegmans's Lectures

Blanning, Nancy, ed. *First Grade Readiness: Resources, Insights, and Tools for Waldorf Educators.* WECAN, Spring Valley, NY, 2009.

Howard, Susan, ed. *The Developing Child: The First Seven Years.* WECAN, Spring Valley, NY, 2005.

Ker, Ruth, ed. *You're Not the Boss of Me! Understanding the Six/Seven-Year-Old Transformation.* WECAN, Spring Valley, NY, 2007.

Lipson, Michael. *Stairway of Surprise.* Anthroposophic Press, 2002.

Long-Breipohl, Renate. "Thinking and the Consciousness of the Young Child." In Research Institute for Waldorf Education *Research Bulletin*, Autumn/Winter 2008, volume 13 no. 2.

Meyerkort, Margaret and Rudi Lissau. *The Challenge of the Will: Experiences with Young Children.* Rudolf Steiner College Press, Fair Oaks, CA, 2000.

Mitchell, David, ed. Waldorf Journal Project #13: *Educating the Will.* Ghent, NY, AWSNA, 2009.

Nuesch, Maria Luisa. *Spiel aus der Tiefe* [Play out of the Depths]. K2 Verlag, Schaffhausen, Switzerland, 2004.

O'Neil, George and Gisela. *The Human Life.* Spring Valley, NY, Mercury Press, 1990.

Olfman, Sharna, ed. *All Work and No Play: How Educational Reforms Are Harming Our Preschoolers.* Praeger Publishers, Westport, CT, 2003.

Patzlaff, Rainer. *Childhood Falls Silent.* Steiner Schools Fellowship, UK, 2007 (distributed by WECAN).

Schad, Wolfgang. *Man and Mammal.* Waldorf Press, New York, 1977.

Schoorel, Edmund. *The First Seven Years: Physiology of Childhood.* Rudolf Steiner College Press, Fair Oaks, CA, 2004.

Rudolf Steiner: *Balance in Teaching* [1920]. Anthroposophic Press, 2007.

_____. *Broken Vessels* [1924]. Anthroposophic Press, 2003. Formerly translated as *Pastoral Medicine.*

_____. *The Education of the Child* [1907]. Anthroposophic Press, 1996.

_____. *The Guardian of the Threshold* [1911], in *Four Mystery Dramas.* SteinerBooks, 2007.

_____. *Harmony of the Creative Word* [1923]. Rudolf Steiner Press, London, 2001. Formerly translated as *Man as Symphony of the Creative Word.*

_____. *Human Values in Education* [1924]. SteinerBooks, 2004.

_____. *A Modern Art of Education* [1923]. Anthroposophic Press, 2004.

_____. "Self-Education in the Light of Spiritual Science" [1912]. Mercury Press, Spring Valley, NY.

_____. *Soul Economy* [1921-1922]. Anthroposophic Press, 2003.

_____. *The Spiritual Guidance of the Individual and Humanity* [1911]. Anthroposophic Press, 1991.

_____. *Study of Man* [1919]. Rudolf Steiner Press, London, 2004. Also available as *The Foundations of Human Experience* (SteinerBooks, 1996).

Dr. Karnow's Lectures

Köhler, Henning. *Difficult Children: There Is No Such Thing.* AWSNA, 2004.

Lievegoed, Bernard, *Phases of Childhood.* Floris, Edinburgh, 2005.

Schoorel, Edmund. *The First Seven Years: A Physiology of Childhood.* Rudolf Steiner College Press, Fair Oaks, CA, 2004.

Steiner, Rudolf. *Cosmic Memory* [1904]. SteinerBooks, 2006.

_____. *Education for Special Needs: The Curative Education Course* [1924]. Rudolf Steiner Press, London, 1998.

_____. "Self-Education in the Light of Spiritual Science" [1912]. Mercury Press, Spring Valley, NY.

_____. *Riddles of the Soul* [1917]. SteinerBooks, 2009.

_____. *Soul Economy* [1921-1922]. Anthroposophic Press, 2003.

_____. *Study of Man* [1919]. Rudolf Steiner Press, London, 2004. Also available as *The Foundations of Human Experience* (SteinerBooks, 1996).

Steiner, Rudolf and Ita Wegman. *Fundamentals of Therapy* [1925] Mercury Press, Spring Valley, NY. Also translated as *Extending Practical Medicine*.

Biographical Notes

Johanna Steegmans, MD, is an anthroposophical medical doctor with a special interest in early childhood development. She is active in Waldorf early childhood teacher training at the Sound Circle Center in Seattle, WA, and lectures and offers courses throughout North America and internationally.

Gerald Karnow, MD, works as a physician within the Rudolf Steiner Fellowship Community, an intergenerational center for the care of the elderly, in Chestnut Ridge, New York. He also serves as school doctor at Green Meadow Waldorf School and works directly with the students of the Otto Specht School.

Nancy Blanning has been active in Waldorf early childhood education for over 25 years, most recently as the therapeutic support teacher at the Denver Waldorf School. She is also a teacher trainer, mentor, and remedial consultant to other Waldorf schools. She serves as the editor of *Gateways*, the newsletter of the Waldorf Early Childhood Association of North America, and is a WECAN board member.